Edexcel AS History Unit 1

Stalin's Russia 1924-1953

Robin Bunce and Laura Gallagher

Series editors: Derrick Murphy and Angela Leonard

STUDENT BOOK

A PEARSON COMPANY

Contents   Stalin's Russia

Introduction

Welcome to History at AS level. History is a fascinating subject, concerned with the world as it was and how it became the world we know now. By studying history, you will encounter new people, new places, new societies and cultures – even though they are all in the past! If you have an enquiring mind and an interest in the world around you then History is the subject for you.

How to make the most of the course

- Practise your skills. History is not just about learning information or about telling the story of what happened in the past. You need to be able to understand and explain *why* things turned out the way they did and about how much they changed. The skills builder sections in this book will help you do this.

- Prepare for debate and discussion! Historians do not always agree about why events or developments in the past happened, or about their importance – so don't be afraid to debate with your teacher and other students. But remember that you must give evidence to support any point you make.

- Use the course book. This book has been designed to help you build up the skills, knowledge and understanding to help you do well in your exam – so use it! See the 'How this book will help you' section for details.

- Read around the subject. The more you learn about a period of history, the more interesting it becomes. Further reading on your chosen topics will broaden your understanding of the period, give you better insights into causation and change and make the course much more rewarding.

What you will learn

Unit 1 focuses on historical themes in breadth. This means that you need to be able to understand and explain why things changed over a fairly long period of time. In Option D4 you will learn about how and why the USSR changed during the rule of Joseph Stalin. You will examine how the man who was once described as 'a grey blur' rose above other contenders to become the ruler of the world's first communist state. You will find out about how Stalin's policies of agricultural collectivisation and rapid industrialisation transformed the Soviet economy and society. You will explore the consequences and costs of Stalin's rule, including the infamous Great Terror. You will see how the cult of personality and Stalin's social policies affected Soviet society and culture – often in unexpected ways. Finally you will discover how the USSR won World War Two and emerged as a global superpower with influence far beyond its borders.

How you will be assessed

For Unit 1, you will take a written exam. You will write two essays, one on each topic you have studied (i.e. one on Stalin's Russia and one on your other chosen topic). For each topic you will have a choice of two questions. You will have one hour and 20 minutes in total, or 40 minutes for each essay.

How this book will help you

- Clearly written text gives you the historical information you need for this topic in the right amount of depth.

- 'Take note' boxes indicate when you should make notes of your own. These notes will help you with the activities and can also form the basis of your revision so it's worth keeping up to date with these as you go along.

- Activities help you understand the content and build up your historical skills.

- Skills builder sections help you develop the essential skills you need to do well in your exam.

- Examzone tells you what you need to know to prepare for the exam, including:

— What to expect on the day

— How to revise

— What the assessment objectives mean and how you can meet them

— What the different levels mean and how you can gain a high mark

— Example essays with examiner commentaries to help you understand what the examiners are looking for and how to use your information.

Chapter 1 **Russia before Stalin**

Key questions

- What systems of government preceded Stalin?
- Why did Lenin want to establish a new government in Russia?
- What were the key features of Communist government in Russia between 1917 and 1924?

Any tourist to Russia will inevitably see Matryoshka dolls, often known as 'Russian dolls'. These dolls come in sets, consisting of several dolls of decreasing size but identical shape, which nest inside one another. In Russian folklore, Matryoshka dolls are a **metaphor** for historical events and processes. Rather than history being a series of revolutions – in which something old is replaced by something completely new, history is like a set of dolls which are essentially very similar. Look closely at one period and you will see the key characteristics of the period that led to it. In this way, Leninism lurks beneath the surface of Stalinism, and beneath the surface of Leninism lies the Tsar. From this point of view, the key to understanding the present is to understand the past, so the key to understanding Stalin is to understand the people and events that preceded him.

Timeline

1894	November: Nicholas II becomes Tsar of Russia
1903	August: The Social Democratic Party splits: formation of the Bolsheviks
1905	The 1905 Revolution
1914	August: Russia joins the First World War
1917	February: February Revolution: the Tsar abdicates March: Formation of the Provisional Government April: Lenin returns from exile October: October Revolution: the Bolsheviks seize power December: Cheka established
1918	March: Treaty of Brest-Litovsk: Russia surrenders to Germany and withdraws from the First World War The Bolshevik Party changes its name and becomes the Communist Party June: Beginning of the Civil War and War Communism
1921	January: End of the Civil War March: The Red Army crushes the Kronstadt Rebellion March: Introduction of the NEP July: The Red Army crushes the Tambov Rebellion
1922	December: The creation of the USSR – the Union of Soviet Socialist Republics

Matryoshka dolls of Tsar Stalin (left), Lenin (middle), and Nicholas II (right)

Russia's geography and people

Tsarist Russia was the largest land empire in modern history. Over four thousand miles separate Vladivostok in the east from Russia's western border, and it is over two thousand miles from the shores of the Black Sea to

> ### Glossary: Metaphor
>
> A metaphor is a word or phrase applied to something to which it is not literally applicable, in order to imply a similarity with something else.

the wastelands of the Arctic tundra in the North. The empire covered over eight million square miles – more than twice the size of the United States of America.

The majority of Russia's population was concentrated in the west. By 1914, the population was 165 million. Ethnically, the majority were Slavs – Ukrainian, Russian or Belorussian. The majority of the population were Christians and members of the Russian Orthodox Church, but the empire also contained sizeable minorities. Roughly 5 per cent of the Tsar's subjects were Jews. There were also many Muslims, including Tartars, Tajik and Turkmen.

The USSR in 1922

At the beginning of the twentieth century, Russia was still predominantly agricultural. 80 per cent of Russia's people were peasants who worked on the land as part of small farms. Only 4 per cent of Russians were industrial workers based in urban areas. The middle class, those who owned factories or those involved in trade, accounted for less than 2 per cent of Russia's people.

For three centuries, Russia had been ruled by the Romanov dynasty headed by the Tsar. Unlike Europe's other royal families, the Tsar had absolute power and was accountable to no parliament or court of law. Consequently, the Tsar's subjects had no civil rights.

The collapse of Tsarism

For many years, the Tsars simply ignored, exiled or executed radicals who called for reform but in 1905, a year of revolution revealed the vulnerability of the Tsar's position. By the end of the year Tsar Nicholas II had been forced to concede, promising limited civil rights and an elected Parliament, the Duma. However, new laws soon reasserted the Tsar's supreme power. By 1914 Tsarism seemed secure, and for a short while the outbreak of the First World War rallied Russia's people behind their Tsar.

The strains of war proved too much for Russia's backward economy and outdated political system. Russia had very little industry and consequently was unable to produce the weapons and supplies necessary to fight effectively. Moreover, war production stifled the manufacture of consumer goods, and food became scarce, a problem that was made worse by the number of peasants who were fighting at the Front.

In early 1917, in the face of imminent economic collapse and military defeat, the people of Petrograd and Moscow revolted. The Tsar ordered his army to crush the uprising, but rather than obeying orders, ordinary soldiers joined the crowds, calling for the overthrow of the Tsar. Without the support of the people or his army, the Tsar was forced to abdicate, handing power to a hastily formed 'Provisional Government'.

Take note

Using the information in this section, create a timeline of key events from 1900 to 1917. Three revolutions occurred during this period. Mark each on your timeline, explaining: (a) why the revolution occurred, and (b) how the government of Russia changed as a result of the revolution.

The rise of Bolshevism

In April 1917, Lenin, the leader of the Bolsheviks, returned to Russia. Lenin argued that a new kind of government was necessary. At the time of the Tsar's fall, councils were set up spontaneously across the country. As government broke down, these councils – soviets – took over the management of local affairs. The soviets were highly democratic and represented the workers, peasants and soldiers. For Lenin, the soviets represented a form of workers' democracy that was superior to the elected parliament promised by the Provisional Government. Consequently, he demanded that the soviets seize power on behalf of the workers and peasants.

Initially, Lenin's vision gained little support. However, as economic conditions worsened, and as military victory eluded the Provisional Government, Lenin's call for 'Peace, Land and Bread' became increasingly attractive. By late 1917, the Provisional Government had lost credibility and against this background, Lenin argued for an armed seizure of power. Lenin's audacious plan was carried out late on 25 October, and in the early hours of 26 October Lenin proclaimed the birth of the world's first socialist republic.

Marxist–Leninist theory

Lenin's bold decision to take power in Russia was motivated by a particular ideology (set of ideas) which is now known as Marxist–Leninism. Marxist–Leninism is an amalgamation of the ideas of two men: Marx and Lenin.

The stages in Marx's theory of history

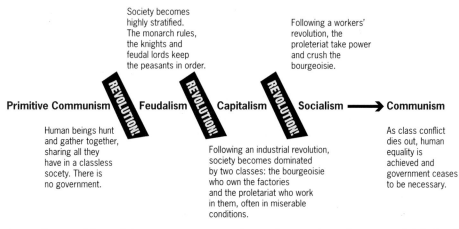

Society becomes highly stratified. The monarch rules, the knights and feudal lords keep the peasants in order.

Following a workers' revolution, the proleteriat take power and crush the bourgeoisie.

Primitive Communism — REVOLUTION! — Feudalism — REVOLUTION! — Capitalism — REVOLUTION! — Socialism → Communism

Human beings hunt and gather together, sharing all they have in a classless socety. There is no government.

Following an industrial revolution, society becomes dominated by two classes: the bourgeoisie who own the factories and the proletariat who work in them, often in miserable conditions.

As class conflict dies out, human equality is achieved and government ceases to be necessary.

According to Marx, history progresses through a series of stages which lead to an 'ideal' stage known as 'communism'. Initially, human beings were all equal and lived together in a condition that he described as 'primitive communism'. However, in order to produce more wealth, a more complex social order was necessary and social classes emerged. These different classes had different aims and interests and were therefore in a permanent state of conflict. In the nineteenth century, when Marx was writing, most European societies were in the process of changing from 'feudalism' to

Bolsheviks and Mensheviks

During the Social Democrat Party Congress of 1903, the party split in two. One faction became known as the Bolsheviks – meaning 'majority' – and the other faction became known as the Mensheviks. The Bolsheviks favoured Lenin's ideas, whereas the Mensheviks rejected them in favour of a more traditional version of Marxism. For example, the Mensheviks believed that the working class would create a revolution on their own, whereas Lenin and his followers argued that the working class had to be guided by a political party. In 1912, the Bolsheviks formally became a separate political party.

Karl Marx

(1818–1883)

A German intellectual and journalist. In 1848 he published *The Manifesto of the Communist Party*, which set out his theory of history, economics and revolution.

Take note

Read the information in this section, and on your timeline, add to your explanation of why the October Revolution occurred.

'capitalism'. Marx believed that a change from one stage to another would be accomplished by a revolution. He anticipated that capitalist societies would be dominated by two classes: **the bourgeoisie and the proletariat**. The conflict between these two classes would lead to a final revolution, which would abolish the class system and create a socialist society. Significantly, Marx argued that only the most economically developed countries would have a sufficiently large proletariat to create a successful socialist revolution.

Marxist–Leninism

Marx's writings predominantly concerned Germany in the nineteenth century. Consequently, it was necessary to adapt his message to Russia in the twentieth century, and Lenin believed that this was his mission. First, he argued that because Russia was a 'backward' country, a revolution would not happen spontaneously. Therefore he developed the doctrine of the 'vanguard party' who would carry out the revolution because the prolerariat were too weak.

In the early twentieth century, Russia was essentially a feudal nation. Many Marxists believed that any revolution in Russia would create a capitalist economy and society. Lenin, however, believed that it would be possible for Russia to miss out the capitalist stage and move directly from feudalism to socialism. He justified this by claiming that the Russian peasants were unusually politically radical and would support the revolution.

The Bolsheviks in power, 1917–1924

Following the seizure of power in October 1917, Lenin and the Bolsheviks attempted to build the world's first socialist society.

Early measures, 1917–1918

Within its first twenty-four hours, Lenin's government issued decrees ending Russia's involvement in the war (later to be formalised in the Treaty of Brest-Litovsk) and giving land to the peasants. Lenin also granted independence to Russia's national minorities. These measures were extremely popular and helped the Bolsheviks to tighten their grip on power.

Other early measures were significantly less popular. In December 1917, Lenin established the Cheka, a political police force who persecuted the enemies of the new government. Press censorship was introduced, initially targeting middle-class newspapers but soon also became widespread among opposition socialist newspapers.

Civil War, 1918–1921

By 1918 the Bolsheviks, who had changed their name to 'Communists', faced a variety of opponents. By mid-1918, these opponents had taken military action to overthrow the new government. The 'White Army' fought to re-establish a Russian monarchy. The so-called 'Green Army' was a guerrilla force of peasants who were fighting for a democratic version of socialism. The Communists also faced nationalist armies representing Russia's national minorities, fighting for the independence that the Communists had promised but were reluctant to give. Finally, Britain, France, the United States and Japan sent forces in an attempt to destroy the new government.

The Communist army, called the 'Red Army' and headed by Trotsky, was highly disciplined and brilliantly organised. The Communists made use of modern technology in order to win the war. For example, Trotsky commanded the army from a mobile headquarters aboard an armoured train. They also set up cinemas to show propaganda films.

War Communism

The economic system that the Communists created during the Civil War was also crucial to their success. 'War Communism' geared the economy towards military production whilst also striving to create social equality. Private property and money were abolished. Work or military service became compulsory, and food was rationed, according to need. In order to achieve this, however, food had to be requisitioned from the peasants. This was extremely unpopular as the peasants received no payment for their produce. Consequently, peasants stopped producing surplus food – and the result was a famine.

It became increasingly clear that the Communists had promised bread, but created a famine; they had promised peace, but started a civil war; and they had promised democracy, but ruled by terror.

The New Economic Policy

In 1921, having won the Civil War, the Communists faced a new crisis. The sailors of Kronstadt threatened military action against the Communists unless democracy was restored and War Communism ended. The Kronstadt Rebellion was particularly damaging because many of the Kronstadt sailors were revolutionary heroes who had supported the Communists from the first days of the Revolution.

Lenin's response was twofold. First, Lenin ordered an assault on the Kronstadt naval base. Over three days, forty thousand Red Army troops slaughtered the ten thousand Kronstadt sailors. Secondly, having put down the revolts, Lenin accepted that War Communism could not continue. At the Tenth Party Congress, he argued that the new government must embrace a limited form of capitalism as a temporary measure. Lenin's New Economic Policy legalised private trade, replaced grain requisitioning with a **tax-in-kind** and, once the economy had stabilised, reintroduced money. Lenin justified this betrayal of communist principles by arguing that it was necessary for the survival of the regime. Significantly, Lenin still refused to give in to the demands for greater democracy. Rather, opposition political parties were outlawed and their leaders were exiled or executed. Additionally, in the name of Party unity, Lenin suppressed debate within the Communist Party by banning factions.

The structure of party and government

It is important to distinguish between the Communist Party and the government of Russia because, although these two institutions were intimately linked, they were not identical. A useful analogy is that of a car and its driver. **The state** or government is like a car. It is a powerful machine, but has no will of its own. The Communist Party is like the driver,

---

Socialism and communism

According to Marx's theory of history, capitalism would be followed by two historical periods: socialism and communism. Capitalism would fall in a workers' revolution in which the proletariat would replace the bourgeoisie as the dominant class. The first period after the revolution is generally referred to as socialism. During socialism the workers would lay the foundations for communism and ensure that the bourgeoisie lost their grip on power. Gradually, as the bourgeoisie weakened, class conflict would disappear, and socialism would become communism. Lenin's aim was to create a socialist state in the hope that communism would naturally follow.

Take note

Study the information in this section. The period between October 1917 and January 1924 can be divided into three stages: early measures, the Civil War and the NEP. Copy and complete this table, showing the problems faced by the Bolsheviks during each period and their 'solutions'.

Stage	Problems	Solutions
Early measures: 1917–1918		
Civil War: 1918–1921		
The New Economic Policy: 1921–1924		

Glossary:

Tax-in-kind

A tax collected in the form of agricultural produce – usually grain, animals, raw materials or labour – rather than money.

Use of the terms 'Russia', 'USSR' and 'Soviet Union'

In December 1922 the Communist government created the Union of Soviet Socialist Republics (USSR), also known as the 'Soviet Union' and – more popularly – by its old name 'Russia'. In this book, in line with the title, we will mainly use the term 'Russia'. However, where the terms 'USSR' or 'Soviet Union' are used, they have the same meaning.

Comintern

The Communist International, or Comintern, was established in March 1919. Technically, it was independent of the Communist Party but in practice it took its lead from the Politburo. Its role was to ferment revolution abroad. Communists from British, German and French parties, for example, attended conferences in Moscow and received funds from the Russian government. Comintern held seven World Congresses between 1919 and 1935.

setting the direction for the car. Consequently, the goal of the Communist Party was to establish control over the state and to use its power to transform society. In countries where several **political parties** compete for power, such as Britain, India or the United States, it is easy to distinguish party from state. But in one-party states, where the state is dominated by a single party for a prolonged period, the boundaries become confused.

The structure of the Soviet state

The October Revolution passed state power to Russia's soviets. Each town or region was administered by a local soviet that was elected by the people. Each soviet elected representatives to the All-Russia Congress of Soviets. In theory, this was Russia's supreme law-making body. In this sense, it was similar to the British or Indian Parliament, or the US Congress. However, as the All-Russia Congress met infrequently it delegated its authority to an executive committee which it elected, called the 'Council of People's Commissars' or the 'Sovnarkom'. The Sovnarkom ran the government on a day-to-day basis, like the British Cabinet. The Chairman of the Sovnarkom was both Head of Government and Head of State.

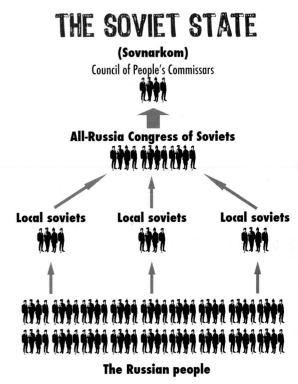

The structure of the Communist Party

The Communist Party was organised into local cells. Each cell elected members to the Party Congress, which met ten times between 1898 and 1921. The Party Congress elected the Central Committee which was, in theory, the leading Party body. However, once in power, the size of the Central Committee – which had around seventy members – meant that it was unable to meet regularly. Consequently, in 1919, the 'Politburo' was established. The first Politburo – elected by the Central Committee and consisting of five men who met on average twice a week during the Civil War – decided important matters of policy on behalf of the new regime.

The 'Secretariat' was appointed to administer the business of the party. In theory, it had no power of its own. In addition, there was an international organisation, known as 'Comintern' (see box).

Relationship between the Party and the state, 1917–1924

As Communist power over the state increased, the Communist Party took over more of its functions. From mid-1918 onwards, the Party became more important than the state, with the Sovnarkom becoming increasingly

THE COMMUNIST PARTY

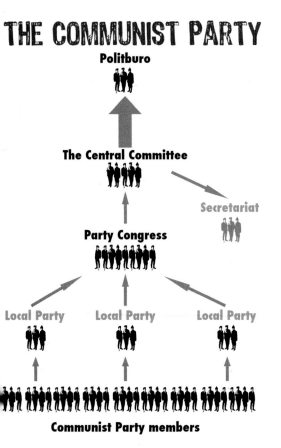

Communist Party members

irrelevant as all important decisions were made by the Politburo.

The Communist Party established control over the Soviet state by outlawing opposition political parties. Consequently, senior members of the Communist Party were guaranteed senior positions in the state. During the 1920s it became common for the Chairman of the local Communist Party to be elected Chairman of the local soviet.

Lenin occupied a unique role in the Party and the state. As Head of State, he was the most powerful figure in Soviet government. However, his real power was based on his personal influence within the Communist Party. Lenin's initiative had created the Communists, his theories inspired them, and his uncompromising determination during 1917 had won them power. Therefore, he alone could unite the different factions and rival personalities that dominated the Party Congress, the Central Committee and the Politburo. When difficult decisions threatened to split the Party and undermine the government, Lenin was able to reconcile opposing views and create unity.

Conclusion

The period from 1900 to 1924 was a period of enormous upheaval for the people of Russia. Nonetheless, a great deal changed in name only. In 1900, Russia was controlled by a single man supported by a ruthless secret police force and a state army. Russia's people were denied civil rights, the press was censored, and opposition to the Tsar was severely punished. During 1917 there was a brief period of liberation. However, by the beginning of the Civil War, the Russian government had reverted to controlling its people through repression and terror. Lenin justified this by asserting that the Revolution must be protected from its enemies at all costs. Nevertheless, by the time of Lenin's death in 1924, although internal and external threats had been removed, there had been no relaxation of the Communists' tyranny.

Activity: Revolutionary propaganda

By 1924, the Communists have been in power for seven years. The Mensheviks have been officially banned and their leaders have been either executed or exiled.

Create a propaganda poster for either the Communists or the Mensheviks. The Communist poster should focus on the achievements of the new government following the Revolution. The Menshevik poster should emphasise the negative aspects of Communist rule. Remember to include as much detail as possible.

Take note

Using the information in this section, (a) list the differences between Party and government, and (b) list the ways in which the Communist Party increasingly took control of the government.

Glossary:

The state

The organisation which governs a nation or a country. It organises national defence through the armed forces, administers justice through courts and collects taxes.

Political party

An organisation which aims to control the state, either through winning a popular election or, in some cases, through a military coup.

Chapter 2   Personalities and powerbases

Key questions

- Why did Lenin's death result in a struggle for power?
- Who were the key contenders for leadership?
- What gave them authority?
- Where did their power come from?

Lenin's death in 1924 created a power vacuum at the top of Soviet politics. Communist Russia had known no other leader. Lenin's power had come from a unique combination of factors. For Communists, he alone possessed the personal authority and the revolutionary stature necessary to lead the world's first Communist regime. Consequently, although other leading figures soon replaced Lenin in various official capacities, none of them could assume his supremacy over Party and government. For this reason, the central problem facing the Soviet Communist Party was how to choose a successor. Lenin's heir would have the historic mission of ensuring the success of socialism in Russia. Yet, in spite of this awesome responsibility, there were no rules and no mechanism for selecting the new leader of the USSR.

Take note

As you work through this information, make brief notes on the strengths and weaknesses of the contenders for power.

Glossary:

vozhd

In Russian, *vozhd* literally means 'leader'. It was a title adopted by Stalin in the 1930s. Unlike the title of Prime Minister or President, it has no constitutional limitations and thus implies unchecked power.

The authority of the contenders

There were five Communists who had a realistic chance of becoming the new ruler of Russia. Their authority – that is, their perceived right to be involved in the highest level of Soviet government – was rooted in their revolutionary record, their relationship with Lenin and their appeal within the Party. Although Stalin was eventually to emerge as Lenin's successor, at the time of Lenin's death he was far from the obvious choice.

Trotsky

Background

Trotsky was born in 1879 into a relatively well-off Jewish family of independent farmers. At the turn of the century, he joined a revolutionary group, but he was soon exiled to Siberia because of his political radicalism. In 1902, following a daring escape, he joined Lenin and other Marxists in London.

Revolutionary record

Trotsky's reputation as a revolutionary was established in the 1905 Revolution. He was a leading figure in the short-lived St Petersburg Soviet of November 1905 which organised a general strike amongst the St Petersburg workers. In 1917, his reputation – and oratory – won support for the Communists during the crucial period in which the October Revolution was planned. Trotsky masterminded the Communist seizure of power and was subsequently responsible for consolidating Communist rule, through his leadership and restructuring of the Red Army during the Civil War of 1918–1921.

Relationship with Lenin

Trotsky's early relationship with Lenin was turbulent and in 1903 he sided with the Mensheviks, rejecting Lenin's belief in a disciplined, secretive, professional political party. These struggles, spanning a variety of ideological issues, continued until 1917. However, when he returned to Russia in the summer of 1917, he joined the Communists and was able to work closely with Lenin. Throughout the Civil War, Lenin and Trotsky also saw eye-to-eye over the controversial issue of restoring discipline to the Red Army. In government, Trotsky acted as Lenin's principal lieutenant and, despite occasional disagreements, Lenin was happy to proclaim that there was 'no better Communist'. Lenin singled Trotsky out as 'the most able man in the present Central Committee' in his Testament. However, he also noted Trotsky's 'too far-reaching self-confidence', a character trait that many others saw as arrogance.

Appeal within the Party

Trotsky's revolutionary heroism in 1905, 1917 and during the Civil War, coupled with his stirring speeches, won him the support of many young Communists and students as well as the loyalty of the Red Army. However, he was not a typical Communist and therefore he had many enemies within the Party. Trotsky's time in exile – in Paris, New York and London – had made him one of the most 'western' of the Party leadership. He was also the most urban. In a country that was predominantly rural and was increasingly proud of its national identity this alienated Trotsky from many within the Party. Finally, many in the Party resented the way in which Trotsky, who had joined the Party late, had Lenin's trust as well as important positions within the government.

Stalin

Background

Stalin, who claimed to be the leader of the world proletariat, was in fact born into a family of Georgian peasants in Gori in 1879. He was educated in a local religious school because his parents wanted him to become a priest. On leaving the seminary, he continued his spiritual education in Tbilisi, the largest and most cosmopolitan city in Georgia, and it is here that Stalin converted to Marxism. He joined the Communist Party in 1902, and in 1912 he was made a member of the Central Committee. Throughout this time, he was continually in trouble with the police, notably for raiding banks to acquire funds for the Party. Activities such as this saw him exiled to Siberia, although he escaped no fewer than five times.

Revolutionary record

Stalin's role during the October Revolution, and the years that followed, was that of a committee member. Broadly speaking, he carried out the orders of others rather than taking the initiative. Nonetheless, he saw himself as a military tactician and he refused to accept Trotsky's authority during the Civil War. Stalin never distinguished himself as a revolutionary hero during this period, but in spite of this, by 1921, his presence on many senior committees secured him a position at the highest level of government.

Lenin's Testament

In January 1923, fearing his imminent death, Lenin dictated his *Letter to Congress*, now known as his Testament (a testament in this context is similar to a will, that is to say a document drawn up to explain someone's wishes in the event of their death). His aim was to point out the dangers of a split in the Party and suggest measures to avert one. He also considered the strengths and weaknesses of leading members of the Party. Notably, while he praised Trotsky, Stalin and Bukharin, he refrained from specifying who should replace him as leader. However, in a postscript to his *Letter* he directed the Party to replace Stalin as General Secretary because of his 'intolerable' behaviour. Lenin attempted to keep his *Letter* secret, asking that it should be read to the Party Congress only after his death.

Relationship with Lenin

Stalin's first recorded meeting with Lenin occurred in 1905. In the period prior to the October Revolution, Lenin came to rely on Stalin's administrative ability and loyalty, and on one occasion even described him as 'that wonderful Georgian'. Prior to Lenin's illness, Stalin was careful to back him on controversial issues. Historian E.H. Carr comments that the 'claim to be nothing more than a faithful follower and disciple of Lenin was not altogether opposed. He had no creed of his own.' Nonetheless, once Lenin became ill Stalin began to oppose him. Lenin was highly critical of Stalin in his Testament, particularly following a disagreement between Stalin and Lenin's wife. He expressed concern that Stalin had 'concentrated an enormous power in his hand' and did not always use it wisely. As a result, he demanded that the other senior members of the party think about a way of removing Stalin and finding someone more tolerant, more loyal, more polite and more considerate to the comrades and less capricious to take his place. Lenin's disapproval of Stalin is also evident in his last essay *Better Fewer, But Better* which was highly critical of the Workers' and Peasants' Inspectorate, of which Stalin was the Head. However, he also recognised that, along with Trotsky, he was one of the 'most able' figures of the Central Committee.

Appeal within the Party

Stalin's appeal was threefold. First, he had the power to advance the careers of those within the Communist Party machine as a result of his many bureaucratic positions. Secondly, unlike Trotsky and Bukharin who adopted extreme positions, he appeared to be the voice of calm moderation. Finally, Stalin, unlike other contenders for power, was prepared to appeal to the national pride of those he sought to lead.

Bukharin

Background

Born in 1888, Bukharin was the youngest of Lenin's potential heirs. His parents were teachers, and he joined the Communists in 1906, organising a strike in a boot factory in the same year. Having been arrested and imprisoned for revolutionary activity many times, he escaped from Russia in 1910 and met Lenin in exile two years later.

Revolutionary record

Bukharin was one of the leading lights in the Moscow Communist Party during 1917 and, following the October Revolution, Bukharin's radicalism inspired his compatriots to seize power in Moscow. During the Civil War, Bukharin's revolutionary zeal was evident in his publications for *Pravda* and his work encouraging German communists to rise up and seize power in their own country.

Relationship with Lenin

Bukharin admired Lenin. In 1916, he wrote to Lenin 'I have the greatest respect for you and look on you as my revolutionary teacher and love you.' Lenin in return referred to Bukharin as the 'golden boy' of the Communist Party. Even so, Bukharin and Lenin were often at ideological loggerheads. Following the Revolution, Bukharin headed the first Communist opposition group, the Left Communists, who criticised Lenin's policy of peace with

Germany. At the end of the Civil War, however, Bukharin abandoned his early radicalism and embraced Lenin's New Economic Policy. In his Testament, Lenin recognised that Bukharin was 'the favourite of the whole Party' and also stated that he was 'the most able force amongst the youngest' of the Party. However, Lenin had serious reservations about Bukharin's skills as a theorist, stating that 'his theoretical views can only with the very greatest doubt be regarded as fully Marxist.' This criticism was highly significant because the Communist Party believed passionately that the correct theory – that is to say, the correct understanding of Marxism – was essential if they were to change the world.

Appeal within the Party

Lenin famously remarked that Bukharin was 'the favourite of the whole Party'. His appeal was such that in 1921 a foreign visitor to Moscow claimed that Bukharin was 'named in Russia as the eventual successor to Lenin'. Bukharin's 'reputation for honesty, fairness and incorruptibility' (in the words of Stephen F. Cohen, his biographer) no doubt explain this attraction.

Zinoviev

Background

Zinoviev, born in 1883, was the son of a Jewish dairy farmer. He was home-schooled and as a result was probably the least educated of the Communist leaders. He joined the Communists in 1903 and, following his arrest in 1907 for revolutionary activities, he was exiled to Switzerland, where he became Lenin's closest collaborator.

Revolutionary record

Zinoviev was undoubtedly short on revolutionary heroism. In October 1917, he opposed the planned coup, and during the Civil War he remained in Petrograd's most luxurious hotel, far from the fighting.

Relationship with Lenin

During his exile, Zinoviev worked with Lenin on a number of books and pamphlets, and returned to Russia with him in April 1917. Their friendship is evident from the fact that Zinoviev then accompanied Lenin into hiding in mid-1917. What is more, their relationship was so close that Trotsky claimed that Zinoviev even adopted Lenin's handwriting. However, following their return, Zinoviev disagreed violently with Lenin on two crucial issues. First, he argued against the imminent Communist seizure of power. Secondly, following the seizure of power, Zinoviev suggested that the Communists should share power with other socialist parties. In spite of this, once he dropped his opposition, Zinoviev returned to his position as one of Lenin's most loyal henchmen. Yet, it was Zinoviev's disloyalty and lack of vision that Lenin remembered in his Testament: 'I will only remind you that the October episode of Zinoviev and Kamenev was not, of course, accidental.'

Appeal within the Party

Of all the contenders for power, Zinoviev was undoubtedly the least appealing. He could be a good speaker when the crowd was with him. However, his vanity, naked ambition and obvious political failings led many in the Party to express their open contempt for him. One said 'after Mussolini, he is the most despicable individual I have ever met'.

Kamenev

Background

Born in 1883, Kamenev was the only potential Party leader who had a working-class background – his father had been a mechanic and engine-driver. His revolutionary career began in 1900 when he was expelled from school for subversive activity. He was arrested and exiled in 1902 and quickly joined Lenin in Paris. He returned to Russia to work for the Communists amongst the working class and was exiled twice more, finally joining Stalin in exile in Siberia. Kamenev's first wife was Trotsky's sister.

Revolutionary record

Kamenev was better known for caution than for revolutionary passion. Following his return to Petrograd in March 1917, he disagreed with Lenin on several issues of strategy, opposing the April Theses, the October Revolution and the creation of an all-Communist government. In addition, he played no notable part in the Civil War.

Relationship with Lenin

After Zinoviev, Kamenev was Lenin's closest friend and collaborator prior to 1917. However, during 1917 he was one of the most senior Communists to oppose the central thrust of Lenin's vision. Following the Revolution, Kamenev was reconciled with Lenin and they remained close during Lenin's final years. In his Testament, Lenin bracketed Kamenev with Zinoviev, reminding his readers of their disloyalty in the crucial months of 1917.

Appeal within the Party

Kamenev had little personal ambition and therefore saw no need to consolidate his support base. In contrast to Zinoviev, he was something of an intellectual, but an uninspiring public speaker. He had a reputation for compromise and for giving up easily in the face of opposition.

The powerbases of the contenders

The authority of the candidates was based on their personal histories and the regard in which the Party held them. However, their power – their ability to make others do their will – came from their official positions within the Party and the government. These **powerbases** were particularly significant because they allowed the candidates to build and mobilise support, or even to use governmental resources in order to achieve their own ends.

Party positions

At the top of the Party stood the Politburo. This can be likened to the brain of the Party – it decided matters of policy and issued instructions to be followed by the rest of the Party. Following 1919, the Politburo, which had fewer than ten members, was effectively the government of Russia. All of the contenders had a seat on the Politburo by the time of Lenin's death, although as a 'candidate member' Bukharin had no vote. On Lenin's death, Kamenev became the Chairman of the Central Committee. This was potentially a highly influential role as the Central Committee elected members of the Politburo.

While the Politburo took decisions, it was the Secretariat that put them into practice. At the Eleventh Party Congress in 1922, Lenin created the

---

Glossary:

Powerbase

A powerbase is a source of power and influence which is based on a position within an institution, such as a political party or a government office.

Take note

As you work through this information, complete the table below, highlighting the powerbases of the contenders in both Party and government.

	Party powerbases	*Government powerbases*
Trotsky		
Stalin		
Bukharin		
Zinoviev		
Kamenev		

position of General Secretary – the head of the Secretariat. Stalin was the obvious choice for this position as he was widely recognised as a superb administrator. In this role, Stalin was responsible for the various branches of the Party bureaucracy. What is more, he was also responsible for interpreting and implementing Politburo decisions. Additionally, the Politburo was dependent on the Secretariat for information and administrative support. Finally, as General Secretary, Stalin gained substantial patronage within the Party because he was responsible for the recruitment, appointment and promotion of thousands of Party workers across the USSR. However, in spite of the power held by the General Secretary, the role was considered to be among the more mundane and unimportant by senior members of the Communist Party.

Stalin was also Head of the Central Control Commission. The Commission was set up by Lenin is 1921 in order to eradicate corruption from the Party. In his role as Head of the Commission, Stalin had the power to investigate and discipline members of the Party. Stalin used this not just to expel corrupt officials, but also to expel Party members who were suspected of disagreeing with him ideologically. Clearly, members of the Party had good reasons for obeying Stalin and ensuring that he thought highly of them.

The Comintern was set up by Lenin to encourage and coordinate Marxist revolutionaries in other countries. Consequently, the Head of Comintern was a prestigious appointment. Zinoviev held this post from 1919, boosting his status and authority within the Communist Party.

The Communist Party of the USSR was organised into local Party groups. Zinoviev and Kamenev were head of the Petrograd and Moscow branches respectively. Potentially, this allowed them to foster support in the two most important cities in the USSR. However, Kamenev in particular was a poor local administrator and therefore failed to earn the respect of the Moscow Party.

Bukharin occupied the unofficial role of Party theorist. Indeed, his book *The ABC of Communism* was considered to be the Communist Party's ideological handbook. From 1917, he was the editor of the Communists' two most important newspapers, *Pravda* and *Communist*. He was also responsible for all city newspapers. This enabled him to influence Party opinion and to deny his opponents access to the press. In addition, he was responsible for Communist educational academies, which were designed to give an ideological education to future Communist Party workers.

Government positions

The Sovnarkom, the ministerial committee at the head of the Soviet government, included both Stalin and Trotsky. Trotsky's most important role within government was as Head of the Red Army. This glamorous and heroic position earned him the respect of young Party members, but it also made senior Communists jealous of the attention he received. Stalin's role on the Sovnarkom was that of Commissar for Nationalities. In this role, he was responsible for overseeing the affairs of all the non-Russians within the USSR, some 50 per cent of the population. Additionally, he was responsible for communicating with senior officials throughout the USSR. Stalin was able to manipulate this position to gain great loyalty from those he was responsible for. Lenin held the central position as Chair of the Sovnarkom, and, initially, Kamenev served as his deputy. In 1922, Lenin offered this position to Trotsky – who refused it, apparently due to his desire to concentrate on writing. Throughout Lenin's illness, Kamenev was acting Chair of the Sovnarkom and was therefore acting head of the Soviet government.

In 1919, the Sovnarkom was expanded to include the position of Commissar of the Workers' and Peasants' Inspectorate. The Workers' and Peasants' Inspectorate – also known as the 'Rabkrin' – was given the task of rooting out corruption amongst government workers. The Rabkrin performed the same job for the state as the Central Control Commission did for the Party. Once again, Stalin was given the power to investigate and expel those working for the government. This increased his power of patronage and ensured that government workers who wanted to keep their jobs would be loyal to him.

Neither Zinoviev nor Bukharin served on Lenin's Sovnarkom. Indeed, in Bukharin's case, Lenin commented that 'we need at least one person with brains without bureaucratic distortions'.

Conclusion

At the time of Lenin's death, there was no obvious leader amongst the senior figures in the Party. Indeed, the government of Russia passed to an alliance of Zinoviev, Kamenev and Stalin, known as the Triumvirate. Kamenev took on Lenin's official position as Chair of the Politburo. Between 1923 and 1924, however, it was Zinoviev who was recognised as unofficial head of the Triumvirate. Yet, the Triumvirate had only come into existence to oppose Trotsky, who seemed to many to be the obvious choice as Lenin's successor. Indeed, a secret British intelligence report of 1925 described him as 'the most powerful figure in Russian Bolshevism'. At the same time, the real power of the Triumvirate lay with Stalin, who was the master of the Party bureaucracy. Nonetheless, Stalin's power was covert and at this stage few in the Party recognised Stalin's influence or considered him a real contender for power. Finally, Bukharin should not be overlooked. Indeed, late in the 1920s Trotsky confidently predicted that Bukharin would shortly 'hunt down Stalin as a Trotskyist' and take the supreme power.

Taking it further

1. What is the difference between authority and power?
2. Which candidate had the greatest authority?
3. Which candidate had the greatest power?
4. Why was the struggle for leadership not simply the struggle to be the Head of State?

Activity: Communist Top Trumps!

Having read through this chapter, use the information presented to complete this table. In each of the categories, summarise the key strengths and weaknesses of each contender for power.

	Revolutionary record	Relationship with Lenin	Lenin's Testament	Party appeal	Party powerbase	Government powerbase
Trotsky						
Stalin						
Bukharin						
Zinoviev						
Kamenev						

You will now use your summary table to compare the five candidates. Award each candidate a score out of ten for each category. Write a sentence justifying the highest and lowest mark awarded in each category.

Using copies of the following Top Trumps cards, fill in the scores in the appropriate boxes.

Play the game! In small groups, each player shuffles their five cards. One player selects a category from their top card and reads out its value. Each other player then reads out the value of the same category from their top card. The player with the highest value in the specified category wins all of the cards played in that round. Continue until one player has won all of the cards.

Having played the game, consider which of the candidates is the strongest overall contender for power. This should emerge through the game as one card 'trumps' all others. Secondly, consider which areas the candidates are strongest in and where their vulnerabilities lie.

Drawing on these activities and the information in the chapter, write a paragraph explaining who you think is in the strongest position for the role of Lenin's successor. Provide examples to support your points.

TROTSKY
Revolutionary record
Relationship with Lenin
Lenin's Testament
Party appeal
Party powerbase
Government powerbase

STALIN
Revolutionary record
Relationship with Lenin
Lenin's Testament
Party appeal
Party powerbase
Government powerbase

BUKHARIN
Revolutionary record
Relationship with Lenin
Lenin's Testament
Party appeal
Party powerbase
Government powerbase

ZINOVIEV
Revolutionary record
Relationship with Lenin
Lenin's Testament
Party appeal
Party powerbase
Government powerbase

KAMENEV
Revolutionary record
Relationship with Lenin
Lenin's Testament
Party appeal
Party powerbase
Government powerbase

Chapter 3 Ideological conflict

Key questions

- Why was the Communist Party ideologically divided during the 1920s?
- Why was there disagreement about domestic and foreign policy?
- Within the Communist Party, what were the different visions for the future of the USSR?
- In what ways did the contenders for power use ideological conflict in their bids to win power?

A great deal united the five contenders for power in the USSR. First, they all agreed that the important changes brought about by the Revolution had to be preserved. They were united in a common desire to build a modern socialist society in which people worked for the common good and were free from exploitation. Secondly, at a fundamental level, all of the contenders believed that history was moving towards a socialist, and then a communist, society. Thirdly, the contenders were passionate believers that one day the revolution would spread to Europe and then to the whole world. At the same time, they recognised the difficulties they faced creating this society in a war-ravaged peasant country, as they all agreed that socialism was only possible in an advanced industrial society.

In spite of this common ground, the leaders and the Party at large were split over how this vision was to be achieved. For this reason, the contenders used ideology as a tool in their struggle for power. The winner would have to convince the Party that he alone had the correct strategy to protect the Revolution at home and build socialism in Russia.

Take note

As you read through this information, make a bullet-pointed list of the different ways in which Leninism was understood within the Communist Party.

Rival interpretations of Leninism

Lenin was the visionary who had led the Communists to power, and it was his ideas that shaped Communist government until his death. For this reason, soon after Lenin's death, senior figures in the Party began to promote 'Leninism', by which they meant the ideas of Lenin. These ideas seemed to guarantee the ultimate success of the Revolution.

However, there was little agreement about what Leninism was. Lenin's ideas had changed over time and as a result his opinions were not always clear. Therefore, rival groups within the party interpreted Leninism quite differently and there were at least two competing versions of Leninism during the 1920s.

The first form of Leninism focused on Lenin's policies during the Civil War of 1918–1921. During this period, capitalism, money and private property had been forcibly abolished in order to win the Civil War. This was Lenin at his most radical, and it was this **idealistic** face of Lenin that inspired the left wing of the Party.

The second form of Leninism took its inspiration from the New Economic Policy introduced in 1921. The NEP was a time of peace rather than war, and the focus was on education and gradual change rather than immediate revolutionary change. This was the version of Leninism favoured by Party moderates who made up the **right wing** of the Party.

The **left wing** of the Party was represented throughout the 1920s by Trotsky, the right wing by Bukharin. Zinoviev and Kamenev switched from right to left in 1925, and consequently lost credibility with many within the Party. For most of the 1920s Stalin avoided taking extreme positions on any of the most divisive issues and was therefore considered to be in the ideological centre of the Party.

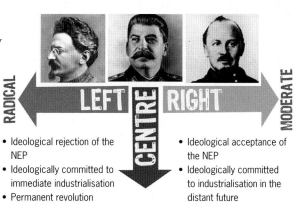

RADICAL ← LEFT | CENTRE | RIGHT → MODERATE

- Ideological rejection of the NEP
- Ideologically committed to immediate industrialisation
- Permanent revolution

- Ideological acceptance of the NEP
- Ideologically committed to industrialisation in the distant future
- Socialism in one country

- **Pragmatic** commitment to the NEP
- Ideologically committed to industrialisation in the near future
- Socialism in one country

The great industrialisation debate

The key problem facing the Communist government was that Lenin's writings were not clear about how socialism was to be built and consolidated in the USSR. Lenin, following Karl Marx, believed that capitalism was necessary to help advance the economy in order for a country to be ready to move to socialism, and then to communism. The October Revolution had created a new government, but it had not turned Russia into a socialist country. Indeed, the Communists had taken power in a country that had only just become capitalist.

In 1921, Lenin attempted to solve the problem of Russia's economic backwardness by introducing the semi-capitalist policy of the NEP. The vagueness of Lenin's view that the NEP would 'last a long time, but not for ever' was interpreted very differently by radicals on the left and moderates on the right.

The left wing – 'the dictatorship of industry'

In 1921, following the famine and devastation of the Civil War, the NEP was accepted by all sections of the Party. However, by 1923 the economy had stabilised. This led Trotsky and other left-wing Communists to call for a radical change in policy. The left of the party argued that the NEP was both ideologically and economically misguided. It was ideologically wrong because it favoured the peasants and returned power to the capitalists at the expense of the working class. This was clearly a betrayal of the principles of the Revolution which was supposed to give power to the industrial workers.

	Left-wing position	Centre and right-wing position
The great industrialisation debate		
World revolution?		
The danger of degeneration		

Yevgeni Preobrazhensky

(1886–1937)

A left-wing Communist economist. He joined the Party in 1903 and during the Civil War was responsible for ordering the execution of Tsar Nicholas II and the Russian royal family. During the 1920s, he was a leading figure in Trotsky's Left Opposition. However, in the early 1930s he joined forces with Stalin, helping to organise collectivisation. Nonetheless, Stalin never forgot his association with Trotsky, and in 1937 Stalin sentenced him to death.

Economically, the NEP was failing to deliver industrial growth. The NEP had successfully stimulated agriculture, but conditions for workers were yet to improve and unemployment in the cities remained high.

To address these ideological and economic problems, left-wing economist Yevgeni Preobrazhensky proposed 'squeezing' the peasants through heavy taxes. The profits raised from this taxation would be invested in heavy industry. Trotsky described this approach as 'the dictatorship of industry'. The primary aim of this policy was to accelerate industrialisation at the expense of the wealthy peasants.

The right wing – socialism 'at a snail's pace'

The right wing of the Party was more cautious. For the right wing, economic stability took precedence over rapid industrialisation. They emphasised the fact that the Soviet government was based on an alliance of two classes – the workers and the peasants. This 'smychka' (alliance) would be threatened by increasing taxes on the peasants. Consequently, the right wing favoured continuing the NEP. Bukharin – the leading advocate of the NEP – suggested that the NEP should last for a period of perhaps twenty years. He summed up this position by stating that socialism in Russia would be achieved 'at a snail's pace'– industry would grow, but slowly.

Stalin's position was similar to the right wing's, but unlike Bukharin he was never a '150 per cent Nepist'. For most of the 1920s, Stalin agreed with Bukharin that the NEP was the correct policy. However, Stalin was always more interested in industrialisation than Bukharin, and never as enthusiastic about rich farmers. Consequently, when the NEP started to fail, he quickly abandoned it. Nevertheless, Stalin refused to ally himself with the left as it would mean forming an alliance with Trotsky. For these reasons, Stalin was in the ideological centre of the party rather than on the right.

World revolution?

Lenin's writings were also unclear about the significance of world revolution. In 1917 he had claimed that the revolution in Russia could only survive with the help of revolutionaries in other countries. However, in other passages he seemed to suggest that Russia might survive and achieve socialism on its own. The first view was adopted by the left wing of the Party, the second view by the right.

The left wing – 'permanent revolution'

Trotsky's theory of 'permanent revolution' suggested that no socialist society could exist alone. Fundamentally, he did not believe that Russia had the economic resources or technological sophistication to complete the transition to socialism on its own. Therefore, Trotsky hoped for a revolution in western Europe, believing that the communist regimes in more advanced countries would then provide Russia with the resources needed to build socialism.

The right wing – 'socialism in one country'

The right wing of the Party presented Trotsky's ideas as pessimistic and defeatist. In 1924, Stalin and Bukharin developed the idea of 'socialism in one country'. In direct opposition to Trotsky, they claimed that the unique character of the Russian Revolution would allow 'the general victory of socialism' in Russia. Moreover, they claimed that this was the view Lenin had held. They believed that the Russian Revolution could be successful on its own because of the smychka between workers and peasants. This alliance made Russia economically self-sufficient and therefore foreign aid was unnecessary. Socialism in one country was highly appealing because it played on Russian nationalism by giving Russia a leading role in world history.

The future of the revolution

Lenin's writings were no clearer on the future of the revolution, and the dangers facing the Party. First, his last writings were highly critical of the growing Party **bureaucracy**. Trotsky and the left wing took up this theme. Secondly, Lenin had repeatedly compared the Russian Revolution to the French Revolution of the late eighteenth century. He had warned that the Russian Revolution, like the French, might degenerate and become a dictatorship. Stalin and his allies shared this fear, seeing Trotsky as a potential dictator.

The left wing – 'bureaucratic degeneration'

The left wing were concerned that the Communists had transformed from radical revolutionaries into government bureaucrats. They feared that bureaucrats who had joined the Party for the main purpose of getting well-paid jobs lacked the revolutionary spirit and commitment necessary to fight capitalism.

Leaders of the left wing set out this view in the *Declaration of the Forty-Six* (1923). The *Declaration* claimed that ordinary Party members had lost their power to the 'bureaucratic apparatus'. Moreover, it stated that those who disagreed with Party policy were afraid to speak out because of the power wielded by this bureaucracy.

In later years, Trotsky claimed that the process of bureaucratisation had been accelerated by the **Lenin Enrolment** which admitted poorly educated workers into Party membership. Trotsky's solution to the problem of 'bureaucratic degeneration' was greater openness and democracy within the Communist Party (see page 25). While Trotsky's proposals were popular on the left wing, they were clearly threatening to the growing number of Communists with good jobs and powerful positions within the Party bureaucracy.

The right wing – 'Bonapartism'

Stalin argued that the real threat to the revolution was Trotsky. Drawing on the history of the French Revolution, Stalin pointed to the danger of a revolution being hijacked by a military dictator. Following the French Revolution, Napoleon Bonaparte – a gifted speaker, intellectual, and a leader of the revolutionary army – had installed himself as Emperor of France. To Stalin, the parallels with Trotsky appeared obvious. Many in the Party therefore feared that Trotsky, like Napoleon Bonaparte, would use his position as Head of the Red Army to become a military dictator. This would

---

Perks for Party workers

The average monthly salary in Russia in 1922 was 6 roubles and 88 kopeks. In the same year, the pay for Party workers was significantly higher. According to *The Improvement of the Living Conditions of the Active Functionaries of the Party*, published in 1922, the minimum monthly salary for the Party Secretaries was 30 roubles in the country and 47 roubles in the city. Party workers with families could receive up to a 50 per cent bonus, depending on the size of their families.

Source 3.1: Stalin on 'socialism in one country'

What do we mean by the *possibility* of the victory of socialism in one country? We mean the possibility of the proletariat assuming power and using that power to build a complete socialist society in our country … To deny such a possibility is to display a lack of faith in the cause of socialism, to abandon Leninism.

Adapted from: Stalin, *On the Problems of Leninism* (1926)

Recruitment campaign initiated by Stalin in 1923 in his role as General Secretary. It was intended to ensure that the Communist Party maintained its working-class character by admitting 'workers straight from the bench'. In three months, 128,000 people joined the Party. Traditionally, workers had had to meet strict criteria before being allowed to join the Party, but Stalin effectively abandoned these rules, gaining the loyalty of many of these new members in the process.

Bureaucracy

A system of administration or management where administrative work is delegated to a large number of officials. In theory, bureaucrats – those working within this system – are only meant to obey orders, but in practice they can gain power and wealth due to their position.

spell the end of the Communist Party and the degeneration of the revolution. Trotsky's statement in 1927 that he would assume the position of dictator if Russia was attacked by foreign powers did nothing to allay these fears.

Conclusion

The ideological battles of the 1920s were extremely important in terms of the leadership struggle. First, each of the contenders had to prove that he was an ideological heavyweight and a true Leninist. Consequently, soon after Lenin's death senior members of the Party published their own accounts of Lenin's teaching, including Stalin's *The Foundations of Leninism* (1924), Zinoviev's *An Introduction to the Study of Leninism* (1925) and Trotsky's *Lenin* (1925). Secondly, the struggle for power was played out in terms of the ideological debate. Stalin, Trotsky, Zinoviev and Bukharin did not attack each other personally – rather they criticised each other's ideological positions. Thirdly, the ideological battles allowed the contenders to win support from the different sections of the Party. Trotsky's ideas were well received on the radical left, as were Bukharin's on the moderate right. Stalin appealed to the centre of the Party, who wanted to protect and advance their comfortable positions within the bureaucracy. What is more, his theory of 'socialism in one country' was highly appealing to Russian nationalism because of the special position it accorded Russia and the Russian people. Trotsky's 'permanent revolution' was vulnerable in all of these areas and did little to win him support. Finally, ideology was crucial to the alliances that formed following Lenin's death. An alliance between Trotsky and Bukharin was unthinkable, given that one was on the left and the other on the right. Stalin, however, positioned in the ideological centre of the Party, could make alliances with any of the other contenders, which strengthened his position greatly. For all of these reasons the common ground that united the contenders was played down while the Party focused on the battle for ideological supremacy.

> **Declaration of the Forty-Six**
>
> In October 1923 forty-six leading left-wing Communists, including Preobrazhensky, wrote to the Central Committee expressing their concern about the lack of democracy in the Party. The document became known as the *Declaration of the Forty-Six*. Although Trotsky's criticisms of party policy were very similar, he was not involved in drafting the letter.

Activity: Communist spin doctor

1. Working in small groups, imagine you are a Communist spin doctor. Your job is to present your position to the rest of the Communist Party as persuasively as possible and discredit that of your opponents. To this end, make a presentation advocating the position of either:

   ● Stalin and Bukharin, or

   ● Trotsky and the left wing.

   Your presentation should include a defence of either 'socialism in one country' or 'permanent revolution', the NEP or rapid industrialisation and collectivisation, and Bonapartism and bureaucratisation. Ensure that your presentation includes a catchy slogan supporting your position!

2. As you watch each other's presentations, consider the following Communist concerns:

   ● Which position appears more Leninist?

   ● Which position appeals more to Russian national pride?

   ● Which position appears more achievable?

   ● Which position will cause less conflict between workers and peasants?

3. In reality, Stalin's doctrine of 'socialism in one country' was much more appealing than Trotsky's policy of 'permanent revolution'. Why do you think this was?

Source 3.2: Trotsky criticises the Party bureaucrats

The centre of gravity in the Party was wrongly centred in the bureaucratic apparatus. The initiative of the Party was reduced to a minimum. Thus, the habits and the procedures of leadership fundamentally contradict the spirit of revolutionary proletarian organisation.

The renovation of the Party apparatus . . . must aim at replacing the mummified bureaucrats with fresh workers closely linked to the life of the working class.

Adapted from: Trotsky, *The New Course* (1923)

Taking it further

Although the focus of this chapter has been on the ideological differences between the candidates, there was also considerable ideological common ground. Using the information in this chapter, list the areas of agreement that were common to all of the candidates.

Much has been written on the ideological debates of the leadership struggle. A useful account can be found in *Stalin and Stalinism* by Martin McCauley (2003). An additional, but more advanced, summary can be found in *Soviet Politics: An Introduction* by Richard Sakwa (1989).

Chapter 4   Shifting alliances

Key questions

- What were the most important alliances and factions formed in the period 1924–1929?
- Why were the contenders for power compelled to form these factions and alliances?
- What was the significance of Leninism and the 'Cult of Lenin'?
- What methods did Stalin use to undermine the power and authority of his rivals?

The events described in this chapter never officially happened. According to official Soviet histories, Stalin became leader of the USSR at the moment of Lenin's death:

Nineteen-twenty four was the first year without V.I. Lenin. The Communist Party and the Soviet people continued their creative work of building socialism under Comrade Stalin's leadership. Comrade Stalin rallied the Party around its Central Committee and mobilised it for the struggle to build socialism in the USSR.

(J.V. Stalin, *Collective Works Vol. IV*, 1947)

However, this is far from the truth. From 1923 to 1929 a bitter struggle for power engulfed the Soviet government. Far from rallying the Party around its Central Committee, Stalin, along with Communist leaders, fought for the leadership, employing tactical alliances, intrigues and political manipulation. Indeed, it was only in 1930, some six years after Lenin's death, that Stalin was publicly recognised as the leader of Russia.

Take note

1. As you work through this chapter, make two lists:
   (a) Ways in which Stalin removes his opponents (including ways in which he capitalises on their mistakes)
   (b) Ways in which Stalin consolidates his own power.
2. List all the ways in which Stalin used Lenin's legacy to gain power.

The progress of the leadership struggle

The leadership struggle is best understood in three stages (see table).

The Triumvirate versus Trotsky and the Left Opposition

Following Lenin's retirement from public life, no single Communist had the power or authority to lead the Party and the country. Therefore, Russia was ruled by a series of alliances. The first was formed in 1923 with the explicit objective of keeping Trotsky out of power. This alliance of Zinoviev, Kamenev and Stalin became known as the 'Triumvirate' or the 'Troika'. But Trotsky would not give up without a fight. During this period, he led an opposition group known as the 'Left Opposition', which proposed alternative policies to those pursued by the Triumvirate.

	Stage 1	*Stage 2*	*Stage 3*
Ruling alliance	The Triumvirate – Zinoviev, Kamenev and Stalin	The Duumvirate – Bukharin and Stalin	Stalin
Opposition faction	Left Opposition (Trotsky)	New Opposition (Zinoviev and Kamenev) United Opposition (Trotsky, Zinoviev and Kamenev)	Right Opposition (Bukharin, Rykov and Tomsky)
Key issues	• The great industrialisation debate • The future of the Revolution	• The great industrialisation debate • World revolution? • The future of the Revolution	• The great industrialisation debate • The future of the Revolution

The Triumvirate had two strategies for denying Trotsky the leadership. First, they would ensure that Trotsky was unable to master the power of the Party. Secondly, they would destroy his influence by questioning his ideology, his loyalty to Lenin and his activities since the Revolution.

Denying Trotsky power

If Trotsky was to take power, he would need a majority in the Politburo. The Triumvirate had been established to prevent this, but almost immediately it faced a problem that threatened to hand Trotsky power. Lenin's Testament had called for Stalin to be sacked because of his rudeness and lack of tolerance. And without Stalin, the Triumvirate would lose their majority, opening the way for Trotsky.

In order to prevent this, Zinoviev and Kamenev argued Stalin's case. They claimed that Stalin had changed and that therefore there was no need to remove him from his post. This argument was accepted by the Central Committee – and Stalin kept his job.

Furthermore, as the Testament was critical of many senior Communists, Zinoviev and Kamenev argued that it undermined the authority of the government and should therefore be kept secret. Once again the Central Committee accepted their argument, and Lenin's words were kept secret. Consequently, the Triumvirate remained secure and Trotsky lost his early advantage.

Having retained his post as General Secretary, Stalin began using his dominant place in the Party's structure in the struggle against Trotsky. First, Stalin drew up approved lists of candidates to be sent to the Party Congress. Previously the local parties had freely chosen who to send to the Party Congress, but this new system gave Stalin control over who attended the all-important Party Congress.

This was a significant advance for Stalin because the Party Congress elected the Central Committee, which in turn elected the Politburo. At the Twelfth Party Congress of 1923, Preobrazhensky was concerned that 'approximately 30 per cent of the Party members are, as one is accustomed to say, "recommended by the Central Committee"'. As time went on, this proportion rose steadily.

Trotsky did little to further his own cause. As a result of poor health he neglected his powerful position in the Politburo, missing important meetings and thereby excluding himself from significant discussions. He also refused to make private alliances with other important Communists, preferring to make his case in public before the Party Congress. This shows that, for all his intelligence, Trotsky did not understand the nature of the struggle in which he was involved. He failed to realise that the real power lay with the leaders of the Party and not with the Party Congress.

Undercutting Trotsky's influence

Denying Trotsky power was a short-term solution. In the long term, the Triumvirate wanted to destroy his reputation, thereby ensuring that he would never lead the Communists. Their strategy involved capitalising on the 'Cult

Lenin's last years

Lenin's health had always been fragile, and by the end of 1921 he was suffering from continual headaches, lethargy and insomnia. He confided in the Politburo about his condition, who recommended an extended period of rest. Initially, this appeared effective, but in May 1922 Lenin suffered the first in a series of strokes. After a period of convalescence he returned to work, making what was to be his last public speech on 20 November. He continued to dictate letters to his comrades until, in early 1923, he lost the power of speech. From that time on he took no further part in Soviet politics. He died in January 1924, aged 53.

Gaining a majority in the Politburo

Since the Civil War, the Politburo was effectively the government of Russia. The Politburo was elected by the Central Committee of the Communist Party on an annual basis. Whoever was to lead the Party and the government would have to be able to count on the support of the majority of the members of both the Central Committee and the Politburo.

of Lenin' by suggesting that Trotsky was disloyal to their former leader and his ideas.

First, the Triumvirate used Lenin's funeral to demonstrate Trotsky's disloyalty. This was easily achieved by Stalin who, according to Trotsky, lied about the date of the funeral. As Trotsky was far from Moscow – and had no other source of information – he did not attend.

Secondly, Zinoviev and Kamenev criticised Trotsky's book *The Lessons of October* for its apparent disrespect for Lenin. They claimed that Trotsky's version of the October Revolution emphasised his own role at the expense of Lenin's. This, they claimed, was further evidence of Trotsky's pride and betrayal of their beloved leader.

Finally, Zinoviev and Kamenev attempted to show that Trotsky's ideology was far from Leninist. Zinoviev invented the term 'Trotskyism'. His intention was to show that Trotskyism was a form of Menshevism and incompatible with Leninism. The Triumvirate emphasised the continual disagreements between Trotsky and Lenin from 1903 to 1917.

It is no surprise, given the efforts of the Triumvirate, that Trotsky and the Left Opposition were defeated at the Thirteenth Party Congress in 1924. The Congress condemned Trotsky for forming a faction against the explicit command of Lenin, who had banned factions in 1921.

The Triumvirate split

Having apparently achieved their goal of defeating Trotsky, the Triumvirate no longer had a common enemy. Consequently, there was nothing to keep them united. Moreover, Stalin was advocating a new theory – socialism in one country – which Zinoviev and Kamenev could not accept. For these reasons, the Triumvirate split in early 1925.

Zinoviev and Kamenev believed that they would be powerful enough to form the new Politburo majority. However, their undignified arguments with Trotsky lost them the respect of many in the party. Stalin, however, had refrained from taking part in these damaging debates and therefore his integrity remained intact. Consequently, when the Triumvirate disintegrated, Zinoviev and Kamenev formed the 'New Opposition', while Stalin united with Bukharin as the new governing Duumvirate.

Duumvirate versus the Left

Stalin and Bukharin needed each other for practical reasons. Stalin was in control of the Party machine, but lacked authority as an intellectual. Bukharin was recognised as the Party theorist and controlled the Soviet media. In combination, they controlled the most important aspects of Soviet political life, having both the power and authority to rule. In addition, their alliance was based on significant ideological common ground. Both agreed that socialism was possible in one country. They also agreed on the continuation of the NEP, although Bukharin was much more committed to the policy than Stalin was. Finally, the Duumvirate was a tactical alliance. Together, Stalin and Bukharin could command a majority on the Central Committee and the Politburo and, in so doing, stop the left from seizing control.

The Duumvirate versus the New Opposition

The first test of the Duumvirate's strength was the battle with the New Opposition at the Fourteenth Party Congress. No longer fearing Trotsky, Zinoviev and Kamenev had felt able to switch from advocating the NEP to demanding immediate industrialisation. They had also criticised the doctrine of socialism in one country. Furthermore, Zinoviev had attempted to contest Bukharin's authority as Party theorist by publishing *An Introduction to the Study of Leninism* (1925).

However, in a debate at the Fourteenth Party Congress they proved no match for the united forces of Bukharin and Stalin. Bukharin easily demolished Zinoviev's arguments in favour of world revolution. Although he was considered 'the outstanding mediocrity of the party' and said little of importance at the Congress, Stalin's contribution to the defeat of the New Opposition was more significant still. Indeed, his role as General Secretary had enabled him to appoint the majority of delegates who attended the Congress. As a result, when votes were cast, the Duumvirate won 559 to 65.

Zinoviev and Kamenev's position was greatly weakened by their Congress defeat. The vote proved how unpopular they were and consequently diminished their authority within the Party. It also gave Stalin and Bukharin the opportunity to strip them of their most powerful positions. Kamenev was immediately removed from the Sovnarkom, and in 1926, neither Zinoviev nor Kamenev was re-elected to the Politburo. In the same year, Bukharin replaced Zinoviev as Chairman of Comintern and replaced Kamenev as Head of the Moscow Party.

Trotsky, who had remained aloof during the debate, did not escape the consequences of the Left's defeat. In 1925, in response to fears that he would become a Bonapartist military dictator, he was forced to resign as Head of the Red Army. This event stripped him of his single most important powerbase within the Party.

Trotsky returns

During 1926 and 1927, the NEP encountered new problems. From mid-1926, Russia's industry could produce no additional goods to satisfy the increasingly wealthy peasants. The lack of industrial goods meant that the peasants had no incentive to sell their grain as there was nothing on which to spend their profits. The result of this '**kulak** grain strike' was food shortages in the major cities and rising grain prices. The atmosphere of crisis was further heightened by rumours that Germany was preparing to declare war on Russia. The crisis reinvigorated the Left, persuading them that it was their duty to fight for a change of policy. Additionally, the threat of war brought Trotsky back from his self-imposed retirement.

Zinoviev and Kamenev now feared Stalin and Bukharin more than Trotsky. Furthermore, their ideological shift from supporting the NEP to demanding rapid industrialisation gave them a sound reason to ally with Trotsky. Additionally, Zinoviev, Kamenev and Trotsky were united in rejecting the doctrine of socialism in one country, in favour of world revolution. Together, they formed the 'United Opposition' and their hopes were high – Kamenev

The Cult of Lenin

'Leninism' was defined as strict adherence to the ideas of Lenin. The Cult of Lenin was much broader and designed to appeal to Russians who had little grasp of political ideology and therefore could not be expected to embrace the complexities of Leninism. At the time of Lenin's death, the Politburo, in an attempt to stabilise the new regime, attempted to turn Lenin into a figure that symbolised the hopes and aspirations of the regime. The Cult reworked religious imagery from the Russian Orthodox tradition, replacing the traditional saints with images of Lenin. For example, Lenin was often portrayed with a halo-like glow. Additionally, Lenin's body was embalmed and kept on permanent display in Moscow and became a place of pilgrimage. Members of the Politburo hoped that the deification of Lenin would put an end to criticism of the Party.

Glossary: Kulak

The Communists distinguished between different types of peasants. Kulaks, according to the Communists, were characterised by their ownership of large farms and their comparative wealth. The fact that they employed other people to work on their land led the Communists to label them as capitalists.

stated that the Party would appoint a new leadership as soon as they saw Trotsky and Zinoviev united. Their position was strengthened by the apparent failure of the NEP.

Kamenev's hopes were dashed, however, at the Fifteenth Party Congress of 1927. Ten years after the October Revolution, Trotsky, Zinoviev and Kamenev were expelled from the Party. In contrast to the defeat of the New Opposition, the expulsion of the United Opposition can be attributed solely to Stalin's growing power within the Party. As in 1925, Stalin packed the Congress with loyal supporters. Additionally, he used his position as Head of the Central Control Commission to formally discipline his opponents for advocating Trotskyist policies and departing from Leninism.

Zinoviev and Kamenev publicly apologised for their ideological 'crimes' and were readmitted to the Party – but their authority had been shattered. Trotsky refused to apologise and was sent into exile. Three of the five contenders for power had now been eliminated. The final battle for supremacy was between Stalin and Bukharin.

Stalin versus Bukharin and the Right Opposition

In 1928, Stalin rejected the NEP and in so doing ended his alliance with Bukharin. Following this, Bukharin appeared to be in the stronger position. He was unrivalled as Party theorist, he had control of both the Soviet media and education, and he was still considered the favourite of the Party. He also enjoyed the support of two senior members of the Politburo – Tomsky and Rykov. Stalin, on the other hand, lacked distinction. He was often referred to as 'Comrade Card-Index' or the 'Grey Blur'. Nonetheless, it was Stalin's adoption of left-wing economic policy, his mastery of the Party machine, his growing ideological prestige and his devious tactical manoeuvring that assured his victory.

Stalin's break with the NEP

Stalin's commitment to the NEP had always depended on its success. Once the NEP began to fail, he pragmatically turned to the left and is so doing broke his alliance with Bukharin. From early 1928, Stalin advocated rapid industrialisation and agricultural collectivisation – the very policies he had previously condemned. His swing to the left was also tactical. With the removal of Zinoviev, Kamenev and Trotsky, supporters of the Left had no leaders. By positioning himself on the Left, Stalin was assured of the support of those who opposed the right-wing policies of Bukharin and his appointees. Moreover, by adopting radical economic ideas similar to War Communism, Stalin was able to appeal to the heroic aspirations of many Communists who had never been fully reconciled to the moderation of the NEP.

Clash of the powerbases

Bukharin's power rested on his control of the Soviet media. Through various official publications, Bukharin could advocate his own policies whilst discrediting his opponents. His alliance with Tomsky gave him considerable power in Russia's trade unions. Rykov was also an important ally, because he was Head of State.

Stalin's powerbase was located at the heart of the Party. Essentially, his power stemmed from his ability to manipulate appointments and promotions within the Party, and fill the Party Congress with his supporters. Crucially, as General Secretary, Stalin also had the right to issue official directives to every Party member. These were central to creating opinion within the Party and allowed Stalin to undercut the influence that Bukharin exercised through the media.

Ideological battle

For many years, Bukharin had been recognised as the official theorist of the Party. However, as the NEP encountered increasing problems, Bukharin's theoretical prestige diminished. Stalin, on the other hand, was growing in ideological stature. The *Foundations of Leninism*, Stalin's contribution to Party ideology, was widely read by new recruits to the Party. Its great virtue was that it was short, simple and easy to read. In this sense it was the perfect ideological handbook for those who had signed up to Stalin's 'Lenin Enrolment'.

Stalin also attempted to undermine Bukharin by resurrecting his frequent disagreements with Lenin. He made sure that every instance of disagreement was republished and discussed in the media. As a result, Bukharin's reputation as a Leninist was undermined. In turn, Bukharin accused Stalin of turning the Party into a bureaucracy. Stalin defended himself by accusing Bukharin of Trotskyism – for the simple reason that Trotsky had been the first to make this claim about bureaucracy.

Tactical manoeuvring

Stalin had little integrity – he was quite prepared to use underhand and dishonourable tactics in his bid for power. Bukharin described him as 'an unprincipled intriguer who subordinates everything to his appetite for power', claiming that 'at any given moment he will change his theories in order to get rid of someone'.

First, Stalin knew when to retreat. In February 1928, he began his campaign against Bukharin by attacking Bukharin's followers at lower levels of the Party. When he encountered resistance, he immediately backed down. Similarly, when Bukharin won a victory against Stalin at the Central Committee meeting in April, Stalin temporarily stopped his policy of emergency grain requisitioning. Secondly, Stalin was excellent at manipulating the Party. To this end, he circulated false rumours that he was about to form an alliance with Zinoviev and Kamenev. In response, Bukharin arranged a secret meeting with Zinoviev and Kamenev. Stalin used this meeting as evidence of Bukharin's factionalism, stating that 'Bukharin is guilty of treacherous conduct'. Thirdly, Stalin was extremely devious. For example, in order to prevent Bukharin attending an important meeting, he arranged for the plane on which Bukharin was travelling to be delayed (twice) in order to allow Bukharin to undergo 'medical checks'. Finally, Stalin ignored Politburo and Central Committee policy and acted on his own authority. In this way, he restarted his policy of emergency grain requisitioning less than a month after it was condemned by the Central Committee. This sabotaged the NEP – and with it, Bukharin's reputation.

Tomsky

(1880–1936)

Tomsky joined the Communist Party in 1904 and was involved in the 1905 Revolution and the February and October Revolutions of 1917. His influence in Communist Russia stemmed from the fact that he was the General Secretary of the Red International of Labour Unions. During the late 1920s, he supported Bukharin and the NEP and was an important ally within the Politburo.

Rykov

(1881–1938)

Rykov was a member of the Communist Party from its earliest days. Following the Revolution, he became a senior economist and chairman of the Supreme Economic Council (Vesenkha). Following Lenin's death, he became one of the most senior members of the Party and government as Head of State and member of the Politburo. His support for Bukharin was based on their common belief in the NEP.

NEP timeline

1921	March: Introduction of the NEP
1923	Peak of the 'Scissors Crisis' – industrial prices significantly higher than agricultural prices – and the government responds by reducing the price of industrial goods
1925	Tax-in-kind is replaced by monetary tax
1926	Agricultural and industrial production restored to pre-First World War levels
1927	Industrial production plateaus. Effectiveness of the NEP is seen to have reached a peak
1928	Grain crisis – peasants refuse to sell grain in an attempt to force the price to increase. Stalin orders a return to grain requisitioning as an emergency measure
1929	April: End of the NEP

Taking it further

1. In the previous chapter, you considered the ideological debates within the Communist Party during the 1920s. How were ideological disagreements used in order to establish the supremacy of the ruling alliances and, finally, of Stalin himself?
2. Using the evidence in this chapter, how far do you agree that Stalin's success was the result of a long-term plan?

Bukharin was a much less able tactician, and he was consistently wrong-footed by Stalin's deviousness. In the early stages of the conflict, Bukharin was keen to negotiate with Stalin in private and therefore refused to condemn him publicly. At the same time, Bukharin chose to work within the framework of the Party rules, giving Stalin the opportunity to disseminate his ideas by allowing him access to the media. Even when Bukharin adopted deceitful methods, he had little success. For example, when he used Lenin's Testament against Stalin, he was condemned – because the Central Committee had previously ruled that the Testament should be kept secret.

Conclusion

Stalin's victory over Bukharin was formalised in a meeting of the Central Committee in April 1929. On Stalin's recommendation, Bukharin was forced to admit his 'political errors' and recognise the necessity of forced industrialisation and collectivisation. However, this was not enough for Stalin. Stalin's economic policies were highly unpopular and he worried that Bukharin would provide a focus for opposition. Consequently, between April and November 1929, Stalin conducted a vigorous campaign against Bukharin in the Soviet press. As a result, Bukharin was removed from all of his important posts within the Communist Party, culminating in his expulsion from the Politburo.

Stalin was an unlikely heir to Lenin. Zinoviev and Kamenev had been Lenin's best friends and closest collaborators. Trotsky was the best known of Lenin's lieutenants, and Bukharin was the 'favourite of the whole Party' as well as the Party's official theorist. But it was Stalin who thrived in the bureaucratic and treacherous environment that Lenin had left behind. For these reasons it was Stalin who won the right to impose his vision of socialism on the USSR.

Activity: Power struggle card-sort

1. Make copies of the following cards:

Forms alliances	Breaks alliances	Keeps Lenin's Testament secret	Prevents opponents from attending important events
Makes accusations of disloyalty to Lenin	Initiates the Lenin Enrolment	Fills the Party Congress with his own supporters	Gives a passionate speech at Lenin's funeral
Makes accusations of factionalism	Supports the NEP	Rejects the NEP	Develops the doctrine of 'socialism in one country'
Removes his opponents from important positions within the Party	Makes accusations of Trotskyism	Expels opponents from the Communist Party	Makes accusations of Bonapartism
Manipulates appointments within the Party	Forces opponents to admit 'errors'		

2. These cards describe methods used by Stalin to win the leadership struggle. Sort them into the following categories:

   ◗ Methods used against Trotsky

   ◗ Methods used against Bukharin

   ◗ Methods used against Zinoviev and Kamenev.

   In some cases, the same card will fit in more than one category.

3. Discuss: To what extent did Stalin use the same methods to destroy all of his opponents? How did his methods change over time?

4. Now sort the cards into the following categories:

   ◗ Ideological methods

   ◗ Manipulation of the Party machine

   ◗ Devious tactics.

5. Discuss: How far do you agree that Stalin's ability to manipulate the Party machine was the key to his success in the leadership struggle?

Skills Builder 1: **Writing in paragraphs**

In the examination you will have to write an essay-style answer on this topic, in approximately 40 minutes. When producing an essay-style answer, it is important that you write in paragraphs. You will need to make a number of points to build up your argument so that it answers the question you have been asked. You should write a paragraph to address each point.

What should you include in a paragraph?

In a paragraph you should:

- Make a point to support your argument and answer the question.
- Provide evidence to support your point.
- Explain how your evidence supports your point.
- Explain how your points relate to the essay question.

Remember: POINT – EVIDENCE – EXPLANATION

It is important that you construct your answer this way. If you just 'tell a story' in which you produce factual knowledge without explanation in relation to the question, you will not get high marks.

An example

Here is an example of a question asking you to produce not a story, but an explanation:

> (A) Why did Stalin emerge as leader of Soviet Russia?

The information to answer this question can be found in Section 1. The reasons you could include are:

- Institutional factors – the position of Stalin and his rivals within the Party and state
- Personal factors – the strengths of Stalin and the weaknesses of his opponents
- Lenin's legacy – the way that Stalin used and abused the systems and ideas that Lenin had created
- Ideological factors – the different ideas about the future of Russia
- Tactical manoeuvring – the making and breaking of alliances.

As you plan, it is important to have a clear idea about the significance of these reasons. To do this, you must decide which factor was the most important. Your answer should convince the examiner that your opinion is correct.

Here is an example of a paragraph which could form part of your answer:

The most important reason why Stalin emerged as leader of Soviet Russia was the positions of Stalin and his rivals within the Party and state. For example, Stalin's roles as General Secretary, Head of the Workers' and Peasants' Inspectorate and the Central Control Commission allowed him to promote or to sack members of the Communist Party. This meant that Party members were extremely loyal to Stalin because they feared losing their jobs and wanted promotion. His rivals, Trotsky, Bukharin, Zinoviev and Kamenev, on the other hand, only had the power of patronage in small areas. Trotsky, for example, had immense power within the Red Army, but practically none within the Party. In this way, Stalin's Party position was extremely important because it gained him support that the other contenders for power lacked.

This is a good paragraph because:

- It begins with a clear statement which assesses a reason for failure.
- It *prioritises* reasons by stating, in the opening sentence, that this was the key reason.
- The opening statement is backed up by evidence. It provides examples of the ways in which Stalin's role was more powerful than those of his rivals.
- The final sentence links Stalin's position within the Party clearly with his success in the leadership struggle.

Activity: Spot the mistake

Below are three paragraphs which attempt to explain why tactical manoeuvring was the most important factor in Stalin's rise to power. However, although the information in each paragraph is correct, there are mistakes in the way each paragraph is written. Your task is to spot the mistake in each paragraph and write one sentence of advice to the author of each paragraph explaining how they could do better.

Example 1

In 1923, when Lenin had a stroke, he could no longer govern Russia effectively because he could not talk and Zinoviev, Kamenev and Stalin formed an alliance because Lenin was ill. When Lenin died, he had not named a successor so the Triumvirate took over and ruled Russia. But in 1925, the Triumvirate broke up and Stalin formed a new alliance with Bukharin. Zinoviev and Kamenev formed a new alliance too, with Trotsky. However, Stalin's alliance was better than Trotsky's and it beat Trotsky. Then, in 1927, the Duumvirate split up and Stalin defeated Bukharin and the Right Opposition to become leader of Russia.

Example 2

An important reason why Stalin became leader of Russia was his use of tactical manoeuvring. For example, he was very distrustful and had been educated as a priest before joining the Bolsheviks in 1903. What is more, he had been a Bolshevik for a very long time, whereas Trotsky had only joined in 1917. Finally, Stalin insulted Lenin's wife on the telephone which upset Lenin. Lenin informed Zinoviev and Kamenev, but they did not act against Stalin. This shows that Stalin was able to remove his rivals by forming alliances and using these alliances to defeat those who opposed him.

Example 3

Stalin was able to become leader of Russia due to his skill at tactical manoeuvring. For example, in 1923, Stalin formed an alliance with Zinoviev and Kamenev and used this to defeat Trotsky, his main rival. Additionally, in 1925, he formed a new alliance with Bukharin which defeated Zinoviev, Kamenev and Trotsky. Finally, Stalin turned his back on Bukharin in 1928, when he had enough support to rule on his own. Clearly, Stalin's opposition was too weak to take power.

Answers

Example1–this paragraph tells the story of the faction fighting, but does not answer the question.

Example2–this paragraph contains lots of detailed information but it is irrelevant.

Example3–This paragraph is generally well written, but the final sentence misses the point of the question.

Activity: Write your own paragraph

Now try writing a paragraph on one of the other reasons for Stalin's emergence as leader of Russia. The information you require is found throughout Section 1.

Remember to begin your paragraph by stating which factor you are going to address. Make sure that you support your answer with factual knowledge and evidence. Then conclude your paragraph by explaining how the evidence it provides answers the question.

You may find the following steps a useful guide:

1. First decide what point you are going to make. Make sure that the point is relevant to the question you have been asked. For example:

    ○ Stalin became leader of Russia by using and abusing Lenin's ideas and the system of government he had created.

2. Decide which evidence you will use to support your point. But choose carefully – make sure that it is relevant and is linked directly to the point you are making.

3. Write your paragraph by:

    ○ Presenting your point

    ○ Backing your point up with evidence

    ○ Explaining how the evidence supports your point

    ○ Explaining how your point relates to the essay question.

Remember: POINT – EVIDENCE – EXPLANATION

Extension work

Here is an example of the style of question often used in the examination. It asks you to make a judgement about causes:

> (B) How far do you agree that the struggle for power following Lenin's death in 1924 was caused by the ideological differences between the contenders for power?

If you were writing an essay-style answer to this question, you would be expected to select information which helps explain why the leadership struggle occurred and to decide on the importance of ideological factors compared with other factors such as: desire for power, fear of Trotsky, Lenin's reluctance to name an heir and personal rivalry between the key contenders. You may also wish to add factors of your own. Using the steps outlined above to help you, write a paragraph to form part of an essay in answer to the question.

Chapter 5   Building socialism in the countryside

Key questions

- ○ What economic problems were created by the NEP in the late 1920s?
- ○ Why did Stalin launch his collectivisation policy?
- ○ How did collectivisation change over time?
- ○ How far did collectivisation meets its aims?

Since the end of the eighteenth century, European radicals had dreamed of a society where human beings had been set free from the curse of poverty and hard labour. In the society they imagined, everyday life would be revolutionised by technology. Machines would do the hard work and people would have more time for recreation and self-improvement. Moreover, careful planning of the economy would eliminate inequalities in wealth. Rich and poor would disappear, and everybody would have all that they needed. This was the radical vision that Stalin presented to the Party in order to win support over Bukharin in the final phase of the leadership struggle. In practice, however, rather than creating heaven on earth, Stalin's reforms led to famine, poverty and incalculable human misery.

The vision of a planned economy

Marxists, such as the Russian Communists, wanted to replace **capitalism** with a more organised and efficient system. Capitalism is based on a free market, where people are free to trade with each other and make a profit in the process. No one organises the economy, and as a result some people get rich whilst others become poor. What is more, capitalism goes through phases of 'boom' and 'bust'. For all of these reasons, Marxists looked to economic planning to create a more stable, more efficient and fairer system, in which the government organised the economy in order to meet the people's needs.

Timeline

1926	Record grain harvest
1927–1928	Decreasing grain harvests
1927–1929	Grain Procurement Crisis
1928	Voluntary collectivisation drive
1928–1929	Emergency measures – rationing and grain requisitioning reintroduced
1929	November: Decree sending out the Twenty-five-thousanders December: Forced collectivisation ordered
1930	January: Stalin approves 'Decree on Measures for the Elimination of Kulak Households' March: Stalin publishes his article: 'Dizzy with Success' – temporary halt to enforced collectivisation, kulaks leave collective farms
1931	Stalin restarts enforced collectivisation
1932–1934	Widespread famine
1941	100% of farms collectivised

Activity: A cow for a plough!

At the end of the 1920s, many in the Communist Party began to believe that the NEP was unable to produce the resources necessary to help Russia industrialise. In any economy, industry and agriculture are dependent on each other. However, during the 1920s, agriculture was unable to produce enough resources to support increasing industrialisation. This activity recreates the economic conditions of the NEP. It illustrates the problems created by the NEP and therefore demonstrates one of the reasons why Stalin chose to move to a planned economy.

1. Make tokens to represent the following things:

   - cows (make 50 cow tokens)
   - 10 tonnes of wheat (50 tokens)
   - 1 tonne of wheat (50 tokens)
   - 1 gallon of milk (50 tokens)
   - Ploughs (20 tokens)

   - Tractors (20 tokens)
   - 10 acres of land (10 tokens)
   - 50 acres of land (10 tokens)
   - 100 acres of land (10 tokens)

2. Divide into teams of two. Two of these teams run state-owned factories that produce ploughs and tractors. The remaining teams run private farms.

3. The aim of the farmers is to make as much profit as possible, in the form of agricultural produce. The aim of the factory managers is to expand production by employing more workers.

4. Begin the game by distributing land randomly to the farmers, ensuring that some farmers have more than others. Also distribute 12 cows, 25 gallons of milk and 30 tons of wheat, ensuring that the large farms get the majority of these resources.

5. At the beginning of the game, both factories should have 100 workers and either 1 tractor or 2 ploughs.

6. Students should trade tokens in a series of five-minute rounds, each representing one year. During each round, students can trade any of their tokens with any other team for any price.

7. Trading rules:

   - Farmers may buy or sell land.
   - Factory owners cannot buy land.
   - Factories can never employ fewer than 100 workers.
   - Each factory owner must aim to purchase 10 tons of wheat, 5 cows and 10 gallons of milk per 100 workers per year.

8. At the end of each round, new resources should be distributed according to the following formula:

   - **Farms**   For every 10 acres of land, gain one ton of wheat
     + two tons of wheat for each tractor owned
     + one ton of wheat for each plough owned
     For every cow, gain 5 gallons of milk a year and 1 cow.

   - **Factories**   For every 100 workers employed, gain either 1 tractor or 2 ploughs
     For every 100 workers, lose:
     - 10 tonnes of wheat
     - 5 cows
     - 10 gallons of milk

9. If at the end of any round a factory is unable to provide for its workers, it should be placed under new management – that is, the factory owners take over the smallest farm, and the owners of that farm become the factory managers.

10. The game finishes after five rounds.
Having completed the game, answer the following questions:

   (a) Which section of the economy (agricultural or industrial) grew the most?

   (b) What happened to the price of industrial products?

   (c) What problems faced factory managers?

   (d) How was the experience of small farms different from that of large farms?

   (e) In what ways was the organisation of agriculture responsible for holding back factory expansion?

   (f) How could farming be restructured in order to meet the needs of industry?

If you do not have the opportunity to play this game, turn to the end of this chapter to find out the results of the game.

What was collectivisation?

Collectivisation was the process by which Russian agriculture was reformed. Traditionally, peasants had worked on small farms with very limited technology. Stalin planned to merge all the small farms into larger 'collective' farms. These new, larger farms would pool the labour and resources and therefore operate more efficiently. In addition, state-provided tractors and fertilisers would modernise production, again making the operations more efficient.

Why collectivise?

Collectivisation was the Communists' long-term aim for agriculture. However, in early 1929, few Communists could have predicted the speed with which this system would be introduced. Collectivisation occurred because of three major groups of factors – economic, ideological and political.

Economic factors

The autumn of 1926 saw record grain harvests for the USSR. However, the harvests of 1927, 1928 and 1929 were all poorer. The decrease in production forced the price of agricultural products up. Consequently, the standard of living amongst urban workers declined. The decrease in agricultural production also affected the Soviet government. Since 1921, Russia's government had been selling grain surpluses abroad in order to gain the foreign currency necessary to provide resources for

	1925	**1926**	**1927**	**1928**	**1929**
Grain (million tonnes)	73	77	72	73	72
Sugar beet (million tonnes)	9	6	10	10	6
Cattle (millions)	60	63	67	70	67
Pigs (millions)	21	21	23	26	20

Take note

As you work through this information, answer the following questions:

1. According to Marxists, how was a planned economy better than capitalism?

2. What is meant by collectivisation?

3. What advantages would collectivisation have for the economy of the Soviet Union?

Glossary:

Capitalism

An economic system in which individuals can trade freely. The government in a capitalist system does not interfere in the economy and allows individuals to act freely in order to gain wealth.

Take note

As you work through this chapter, complete the following table, comparing Stalin's aims for collectivisation with his achievements.

	Economic aims (add details)	Ideological aims (add details)	Political aims (add details)
Successes			
Failures			

industrialisation. Clearly, if there were no grain surpluses there would be no money to build Russia's industry.

In this context, collectivisation held out the prospect of many economic benefits. First, large farms would increase efficiency. Secondly, collectivisation could be accompanied by mechanisation. The greater efficiency would mean that fewer people were needed to work on the farms, thus releasing extra manpower for Russia's developing industry.

Finally, collectivisation promised a significant increase in production. This would allow the government to sell more overseas, providing more resources for industrialisation and a higher standard of living for urban workers.

Ideological factors

In many ways Communism had done little to change Russian agriculture. Indeed, peasants were still using traditional farming techniques. Additionally, peasant attitudes remained conventional. Their lack of revolutionary spirit was also evident in the way they farmed – rather than producing grain for the good of the community, the peasants produced for themselves and their own profit. These considerations led many Communists to believe that collectivisation was essential if the capitalist peasants were to embrace socialism.

Political factors

Stalin's desire to initiate collectivisation was also motivated by his struggle against Bukharin and the Party's rightwing. The radical nature of collectivisation appealed to the Party's left wing. Moreover, it was far more appealing to many in the Communist Party than the right-wing alternative of importing grain. Grain imports would mean reducing the pace of industrialisation because the money used to buy grain could not be spent on developing Russia's industry.

Stalin's own understanding of agriculture also has some bearing on the decision to collectivise. Although Stalin had a peasant background, he knew little about agriculture. Indeed, he visited farming land on only one occasion in his entire adult life. This visit occurred in 1928 and lasted for less than a month. During this time, Stalin showed just how simplistic his view of agriculture was. He believed Russia's agriculture could be transformed by an act of the will and strong leadership. He also asserted that peasants who refused to cooperate with state agricultural policy were essentially terrorists and enemies of the people, who should be shown no mercy.

The Grain Procurement Crisis, 1927–1929

The Grain Procurement Crisis illustrates the economic, ideological and political causes of the new policy. The Crisis also acted as the catalyst which ended the NEP and ushered in the new era of collectivisation.

Under the NEP, the government bought grain from the peasants on the free market. Poor harvests from 1927 onwards forced the price of grain up. Moreover, the richer peasants – the kulaks – started to withhold grain from the market in order to push the price up further. Stalin described this as the

'Kulak Grain Strike' and used it as an excuse to revive the policy of grain requisitioning. For Stalin the so-called Grain Strike illustrated the fact that the peasant could effectively hold the government to ransom and slow down the process of industrialisation. In addition, the strike demonstrated the fact that peasant ideology was essentially capitalist and therefore in conflict with that of the government. Finally, Stalin used the crisis as evidence of the NEP's failure, and in so doing undermined Bukharin's position on the right of the party.

The course of collectivisation

The Soviet government moved towards mass collectivisation in a series of stages. In many cases a radical policy was adopted, then reversed, only to be reintroduced later when Stalin was in a more secure position. It appears that Stalin had no grand plan, but adopted extreme measures as a pragmatic response to Russia's economic difficulties.

Emergency measures

Stalin's response to the Grain Procurement Crisis was to increase the power of the government over the economy. First, in the winter of 1928–1929, in response to a scarcity of bread and sugar, Stalin re-introduced rationing to the cities. Second, at the end of 1928, the state resumed grain requisitioning. Under Article 107 of the Soviet Criminal Code, grain hoarding could be punished, and Stalin rewarded poorer peasants who informed on their richer neighbours by giving them the land that had belonged to the kulaks. These policies created huge resentment among the peasants, and Bukharin persuaded the Party to abandon the policy. Nonetheless, as Stalin's power grew the policy was restarted. In the spring of 1929, the government started to requisition meat, and in the middle of the same year they revised Article 61 of the Criminal Code, giving the police powers to send kulaks to labour camps for up to two years for 'failure to carry out general state instructions'.

The liquidation of the kulaks

Mass collectivisation began in December 1929 with Stalin's instruction to 'liquidate the kulaks as a class'. Stalin's instruction was significant for two reasons. First, 'dekulakisation' marked the end of capitalism and independent farming in the countryside. Secondly, it vastly increased the speed of collectivisation. Initially, Stalin had proposed that only 30 per cent of Russia's farms would be collective by 1934. However, the call to liquidate the kulaks entailed immediate collectivisation of all farming in Russia.

Stalin appealed to the poorest peasants to lead the way. The new collective farms would control all of the land in the local area, and the peasants would pool their resources. In essence, this meant that the poorest peasants would be able to use the kulak's resources and share in a much greater harvest.

However, the poorest peasants were a minority of Russia's farmers. For the majority, collectivisation meant a loss of independence as well as significant financial loss. Therefore, the majority of peasants rebelled, choosing to destroy grain and livestock rather than surrender it to the collective farms. For example, 18 million horses and 100 million sheep and goats were

Take note

1. As you work through this section, make notes on the key features of:
   - Emergency measures
   - Liquidation of the kulaks
   - The Twenty-five-thousanders
   - Stalin's 'Dizzy with Success' article.

   In each case, list (a) what Stalin did, and (b) how Stalin's policies attempted to solve the economic problems facing the Soviet Union.

2. How did Stalin's policies lead to the famine of 1931?

Source 5.1: Stalin, 'Dizzy with Success'

Everybody is now talking about the success of Soviet power in the field of the collective farm movement. But successes have their dark side. These successes sometimes lead to a spirit of self-importance. These successes sometimes make people drunk, people's heads become dizzy with success, and the sense of measure is lost.

Adapted from: Stalin, 'Dizzy with Success', *Pravda*, 3 March 1930

destroyed between 1929 and 1933. Kulaks also destroyed what machinery they had, rather than allow it to fall into the hands of the Communists.

The Twenty-five-thousanders

Immediately prior to the start of forced collectivisation, Stalin initiated a new policy. Local Communists were unhappy about the collectivisation plans and therefore unwilling to implement them. In order to get round this, Stalin issued a decree sending 25,000 'socially conscious' industrial workers into the countryside. Over 27,000 enthusiastic workers volunteered for this scheme, hoping to revolutionise the countryside and play their part in building socialism in Russia. Following a two-week course, the 'Twenty-five-thousanders', as they became known, were supposed to offer technical help to peasants and instruct them on the use of the new, more complex machinery.

In reality, the Twenty-five-thousanders were used to enforce dekulakisation. The volunteers were expected to find secret stores of grain and confiscate them, round up the kulaks and organise their exile, and force the remaining peasants into collective farms.

'Dizzy with Success'

The first wave of forced collectivisation resulted in untold human suffering. The majority of kulaks and their families were either shot or herded into cattle trucks and exiled to Siberia. On arrival in Siberia, those who survived the journey were imprisoned in forced labour camps run by the secret police, where tens of thousands died of disease and hunger. Publicly, Stalin was unmoved by the fate of his victims and announced 'Moscow does not believe in tears'.

In addition to the human cost of collectivisation, the process caused chaos in the agricultural economy. Resistance to forced collectivisation had resulted in the wholesale slaughter of livestock, the destruction of tractors, and even the burning of crops. Finally, the process of collectivisation created a surge of hostility towards the government. Although Stalin disregarded the human suffering caused by collectivisation, economic and political reality forced him to call a halt to the process in March 1930.

In 'Dizzy with Success', an article published in *Pravda*, Stalin defended his policy but claimed that some local officials had been 'overenthusiastic' whilst implementing collectivisation. He also argued that the target for collectivisation had been met and therefore the programme would be suspended. Stalin never admitted that collectivisation had caused problems, let alone that so many had been killed or exiled, but the article was a tacit admission that many within the Party believed that the carnage had gone too far.

At the time of the article's publication (March 1930), approximately half of Russia's farms had been collectivised. By August, however, many peasants had gone back to their own farms, and by the end of the year only a quarter of Russian farmers remained in collectives.

Famine

The pause in collectivisation was short-lived. Pressure to collectivise resumed in 1931. The result of this second wave of collectivisation was a famine unprecedented in Russian history. Significantly, this famine was the result of government policy rather than natural disaster. In 1931, the government issued hugely unrealistic targets to Russian farmers. Nonetheless, Stalin announced that failure to meet these targets was considered sabotage and would be punished severely. True to his word, when farmers failed to meet their targets Stalin ordered the seizure of grain by the Red Army and the secret police. In order to meet government targets all grain was confiscated. Peasants caught hiding even one or two ears of corn were exiled or shot.

Stalin was uncompromising. For example, as punishment for failing to meet their targets, Stalin set up military checkpoints to stop food entering Ukraine. Trains passing through the region were ordered to keep their windows shut to prevent food falling on to the tracks. International offers of aid were rejected as Stalin claimed there was no famine in socialist Russia. The consequences were appalling. People were forced to take drastic measures to survive, such as fighting over horse manure which contained some undigested grain. The Soviet authorities made no count of the dead, but conservative estimates suggest that at least ten million died during the famine.

As intended, much of the grain that had been seized from the peasants was taken to the cities or exported in order to provide the resources for industrialisation. However, Stalin's economic policy was in such chaos that often grain sat in barns rotting, while peasants starved in nearby villages.

The consequences of collectivisation

Collectivisation was Stalin's method of bringing socialism and economic efficiency to the countryside. In these terms, it undoubtedly failed. It was also linked to industrialisation and in this sense there was some success. Finally, although the policy created economic chaos, famine and massive open hostility to the government, the policy strengthened Stalin's position, and in this way it was a political triumph.

The effect on rural areas

Collectivisation had a devastating effect on the Russian peasantry. Between 9,500,000 and 10,000,000 people were exiled as part of the dekulakisation drive. In 1929, 150,000 kulak families were sent to Siberia. This figure rose to 240,000 in 1930, and rose again to 285,000 in 1931. In some cases, 10 per cent of the peasants in a single village were exiled.

The peasants who remained on the new collective farms endured enormous hardship. They were forced to meet unrealistic targets and paid little for the crops they produced. Most farms were barely able to cover their production costs. Consequently, rather than filling peasants with communist spirit, collectivisation created anger and resentment towards the government. There was little incentive for hard work on the collective farms as the peasants no longer owned the land they worked on and received little reward for their labour. As a result, labour productivity in rural areas declined.

Collectivisation undoubtedly failed to raise agricultural production. The peasants who were exiled were often the hardest working and the most enterprising. Therefore, without their talents and energy, production could

Take note

As you work through this section, make a bullet-pointed list of the effects of collectivisation (a) in rural areas, (b) in urban areas, and (c) within the Communist Party. Divide your notes into general points and supporting specific examples. Do not note down any general points without specific examples, and do not note down any specific examples without linking them to general points.

Machine Tractor Stations

The Machine Tractor Station (MTS) had a dual function. Officially, they were there to provide machinery and training. Their second function was to exercise political control over the collective farms they were supporting. In this capacity, workers at the MTS would spy on the peasants and ensure that troublemakers were dealt with swiftly.

**A cow for a plough!
What you should
have learned**

(a) The agricultural section of the economy grows very quickly and, by the second or third round, wheat has become almost worthless because so much of it is being produced.

(b) Industry grows very slowly. Consequently, industrial goods become very expensive.

(c) Factory managers find it difficult to meet the needs of their workers. Trading with lots of small farms is problematic because none of them have all of the resources necessary for the factory.

(d) Inequality grows sharply. Some farmers become very rich, whilst others can find no market for their goods.

(e) An environment in which there are lots of small and medium-sized farms makes it difficult to provide the necessary resources for industrial growth in an efficient manner.

(f) Overall, the system would be much more efficient if the farms were merged into fewer, larger farms, which were specifically designed to meet the needs of industry.

only fall. The harvest of 1933 was nine million tonnes less than that of 1926. In terms of livestock, the number of horses halved between 1928 and 1932, while the number of pigs dropped by 65 per cent in the same period.

Collectivisation was accompanied by mechanisation, but in the early phase it was ineffective. In June 1930 the Central Committee agreed the creation of a national network of Machine Tractor Stations (MTSs). Because of bad planning, however, the implementation of the MTS network was not really started until early 1931. Additionally, in order to extract more grain from the peasants, the government kept the price of hiring tractors high. Consequently, few farms were able to acquire new machinery. By the end of 1932 there were almost 75,000 tractors and 2,500 MTSs across Russia. However, half of Russian farms were left out of the network. Moreover, the extra tractors did not make up for the loss of millions of horses. Consequently, the MTSs were unable to make significant improvements in the productive capacity of Soviet agriculture.

In one sense, however, the policy was an overwhelming success. In 1930, around 25 per cent of peasant households were collectivised. By 1941, all farms in Soviet Russia were collective. Nonetheless, the cost of this achievement was astronomical.

Industrialisation and urbanisation

One of the goals of collectivisation was to provide more grain for export in order to generate the funds to industrialise. Although the amount of grain produced fell from 1926 onwards, the amount of grain procured and exported by the state increased. In 1928, the state procured 11 million tonnes of grain. This rose to 16 million tonnes in 1929, and 23 million tonnes in 1933. Similarly, grain exports rose from 0.03 million tonnes in 1928 to over 5 million tonnes in 1931.

Although there was no famine in the cities, the standard of living for industrial workers fell sharply following collectivisation. The value of their wages fell by half between 1928 and 1932. Significantly, the amount of meat consumed by urban workers fell by two-thirds from 1928 to 1932.

Collectivisation failed to deliver greater unity between workers and peasants. The government officially blamed 'kulak spirit' among the peasants for poor harvests. This propaganda fed the suspicions of urban workers that the peasants were refusing to play their part in building socialism.

Stalin's agricultural policy did play a part in increasing urbanisation. In 1928, only 18 per cent of Soviet citizens were working class. This figure had risen to 50 per cent in 1939. In some cities, the urban population trebled during the 1930s. Indeed, between 1922 and 1940, the number of Russians living in cities rose from 22 million to 63 million. This created problems of its own, because the government was reluctant to invest in housing in urban areas.

Political consequences

The famine in the countryside and the poverty in the cities created a feeling of crisis in the top levels of the Communist Party. But rather than provoking criticism of Stalin and his policies, the chaos united the Party behind their new leader. Fearing another civil war, Party leaders were fiercely loyal to the new policies, and blamed the kulaks and peasant saboteurs for the problems that Russia was experiencing. Communists on the left wing of the Party also viewed Stalin's hard line against the peasants as a return to the heroic traditions of the Civil War. Therefore, Stalin emerged from the mayhem of collectivisation stronger than ever before.

Conclusion

Collectivisation led to the deaths of over ten million peasants in the famine of 1932–1934. A similar number were moved to forced labour camps in Siberia. Soviet agriculture would take decades to recover. In terms of Stalin's personal ambition, the policy was a success. More grain was procured, more grain was exported, Russia was urbanised, and Stalin's authority reached new heights.

Stalinism is often remembered for the terror of the mid-1930s, when tens of thousands of communists and workers were executed or exiled for being enemies of the state. However, the famine of 1932–1934 shows Stalin at his most ruthless. Indeed, years before the show trials and the terror, Russia's peasantry were Stalin's first victims.

Activity: What could have happened?

1. Think back to the game you played at the beginning of this chapter (A cow for a plough!) which recreated the Soviet economy under the NEP. Under this system:

- What problems faced industry?
- What problems faced agriculture?
- What suggestions did you make for restructuring farming?
- How far were these suggestions in line with Stalin's policy of collectivisation?

2. Form two groups. Each group represents a set of economic policy advisers.

Group 1 represents the Communist right wing, who favour working with the peasants and are prepared to compromise with capitalism.

Group 2 represents the Communist left wing, whose overriding aim is industrialisation, at whatever cost.

3. Discuss the following policies and events:

- Emergency measures
- 'Dizzy with Success'
- Liquidation of the kulaks
- Famine, 1932–1934.

For each, Group 1 must suggest viable policy alternatives, while Group 2 must defend Stalin's actual policy.

4. The historian Dmitri Volkogonov claims that 'the restructuring of agriculture could have been accomplished without terror and tragedy'. How far do you agree with this statement?

Taking it further

Following the fall of Communism in 1989, it has been common to stress the tragedy of collectivisation. However, for Communists at the time, it was viewed as a bold move to modernise Russia. One way in which it is possible to understand this perspective is to watch the 1930 propaganda film *Earth* by Ukrainian director Alexander Dovzhenko. Essentially, the film tells the story of a band of heroic peasants who collectively buy a tractor in an attempt to modernise their farm. However, the tractor destroys the property of a local kulak, who in revenge murders a peasant.

Chapter 6   Organised chaos – the First Five-Year Plan

Key questions
- Why did Stalin introduce the First Five-Year Plan?
- What were the key features of the First Five-Year Plan?
- How successfully did the First Five-Year Plan meet its aims?

Stalin's 'First Five-Year Plan' was not a plan and it did not last five years. Rather, it was a massive propaganda exercise, designed to persuade the Soviet people and the world at large that something amazing was taking place in Russia. Nonetheless, for all its shortcomings, the Five-Year Plan was more than just an illusion. Indeed, Stalin's Five-Year Plans were the biggest economic experiment of the twentieth century, and they underpinned one of the twentieth century's longest-lasting dictatorships. Between October 1928 and December 1932, the Russian economy was transformed, and Russia became an industrial giant. The foundation was laid for the USSR's emergence as a superpower.

Take note

This section considers the reasons why Stalin introduced the First Five-Year Plan. As you work through it, use the information to complete the following diagram:

Ideological causes

Economic causes

Why did Stalin introduce the First Five-Year Plan?

Political causes

Stalin's Five-Year Plans

First Five-Year Plan	October 1928 – December 1932
Second Five-Year Plan	January 1933 – December 1937
Third Five-Year Plan	January 1938 – June 1941
Fourth Five-Year Plan	January 1946 – December 1950
Fifth Five-Year Plan	January 1951 – December 1955

Reasons for the Five-Year Plan

Stalin's aim was to revolutionise Russia by creating a genuinely socialist economy and society. Collectivisation would achieve this in agriculture, and industry would be reformed by a series of five-year plans. Stalin's reasons for launching the First Five-Year Plan were ideological, political and economic.

Ideological causes

Stalin, along with all Russian Communists, believed that socialism was only possible in a highly advanced industrialised nation. However, the Communist Revolution had taken place in an economically backward country which was perhaps a hundred years behind the advanced economies in the West. Therefore, in order to make the dream of socialism a reality, Stalin set an audacious agenda – 'in ten years at most we must make good the distance which separates us from the advanced capitalist countries'.

Stalin also believed that the revolution should serve the working class. Under the NEP the peasants had prospered while conditions for the workers were slow to improve. Stalin aimed to reverse this. He intended to replace the 'bourgeois specialists' who managed industry during the NEP with 'red specialists' who were educated by the Communist government and who came from the ranks of the working class.

Political causes

The belief that 'crash industrialisation' was possible was inspired by the 'successes' of collectivisation. Additionally, having won the leadership struggle, there is evidence that Stalin was no longer content to be seen as Lenin's pupil. Rather, he was keen to develop a reputation that surpassed that of Lenin. In 1929, on Stalin's fiftieth birthday, he made the unusual move of giving a speech about Lenin's mistakes. His message was clear – Lenin's Russia, the Russia of the NEP, was over, and 'Stalin's Russia' was just beginning.

Finally, Stalin was concerned that Russia would be unable to defend itself against capitalist nations in the event of war. In order to repel attacks, Russia would need to develop iron, steel, oil and coal industries on a grand scale, because these were the industries necessary for modern warfare.

Economic causes

The First Five-Year Plan was introduced in response to the NEP's failure to industrialise Russia. Even the NEP's supporters acknowledged that the policy could only industrialise the country 'at a snail's pace'. For example, the amount of iron, steel and copper produced under the NEP never exceeded the amount produced in the last years of Tsarism. Equally, improvements in production of commodities such as crude oil and coal still left Russia significantly behind Germany, France and other western nations. Clearly, the NEP was not producing results fast enough – and a new approach was needed.

The nature of the First Five-Year Plan

The First Five-Year Plan was essentially a series of targets, drawn up by government officials working for an organisation known as Gosplan – the State Planning Committee. Gosplan employed almost half a million bureaucrats, who set targets for every factory, workshop, mill and mine in Russia. The Plan was so extensive that when it was published it comprised three large volumes. All of the targets were set centrally, and in most cases, the officials who set them had only a sketchy knowledge of the factory they were dealing with.

The Plan went through a series of drafts. Indeed, the Plan was continually revised during its operation. The first version of the Plan was drawn up in 1927 and set ambitious targets for industries such as coal, iron and steel. In 1932, Stalin revised the targets upwards, producing two new versions of the Plan. Each revision made fulfilling the Plan more unrealistic. Consequently, as historian Alec Nove has argued, the Five-Year Plans do not deserve the title 'Plans' at all. An economic plan, properly defined, carefully matches raw materials to production, and production to consumption. The first Five-Year Plan, and its successors, made no attempt to do this. Rather, the government demanded production with no clear idea of how it was to be achieved or what was to be done with the materials produced. In this sense, it is more

> **Take note**
>
> As you work through the following sections, make notes on:
> (a) How the First Five-Year Plan was organised
> (b) What the Five-Year Plan was designed to achieve.

appropriate to refer to Stalin's economy as a 'command economy' – a system based on a series of central orders – rather than as a 'planned' economy.

The priorities of the First Five-Year Plan

The First Five-Year Plan explicitly favoured heavy industry – iron, coal, steel and oil – over consumer goods such as textiles and food.

Stalin's priorities

Stalin's understanding of industry was as unsophisticated as his understanding of agriculture. In Stalin's mind, industrialisation equated to the creation of heavy industry. While he only visited farmland once in his entire career, he regularly visited iron foundries and steelworks. He described coal, steel and oil as the 'basic, decisive branches of industry'. For Stalin, these industries were 'decisive' because they were the first industries developed in the nineteenth-century industrial revolution. Therefore, Stalin believed that if he was to take Russia down the path of industrialisation, he had to start with these heavy industries. Additionally, Stalin prized physical and mental strength and had little time for the 'bourgeois luxury' of an easy life. This aspect of his character is clearly reflected in his adopted name – Stalin literally means 'man of steel'. Stalin's obsession with heavy industry was bound up with his desire to create a strong Russia, a country of iron and steel.

A communist poster from 1932. It says 'Komsomol members fight for the Bolsheviks' reconstruction of transport!'

Foundational industries

The focus on heavy industry was, in part, an attempt to lay the foundation for future industrial development. All industries needed raw materials such as coal, steel, oil and iron in order to develop. Moreover, the mass production of raw materials was also foundational in a second sense. The majority of Stalin's industrial labour force were unskilled peasants who had only recently left the countryside following collectivisation. Unskilled peasants were poorly suited to the production of complex consumer goods, but they were well matched to the production of large quantities of raw materials. Stalin's planners believed that, over time, working in heavy industry would allow the peasants to gain the skills necessary to work in more sophisticated industries, such as textiles. Thirdly, heavy industry would lay the foundation for rearmament in the case of war. While Stalin was not intending to create a war economy during the First Five-Year Plan, he was undoubtedly concerned that Russia should be ready to defend itself in the event of invasion.

Successes of the First Five-Year Plan

In December 1932, Stalin announced that the First Five-Year Plan had been such a success that it was to finish a year early. Certainly, there were some successes. The production of raw materials had increased substantially, and in some ways, Russia was a more dynamic society.

Increasing production

By conservative estimates, the First Five-Year Plan caused the Russian economy to grow at around 14 per cent a year. This is a remarkable achievement, particularly in the context of the international economy. America and Europe were in a state of depression following the Wall Street crash.

The First Five-Year Plan was also impressive compared with the economic achievements of Tsarism and the NEP. In terms of iron, steel, coal and oil, the First Five-Year Plan outperformed any previous economic system (see table).

Take note

Referring to the spider diagram that you completed at the beginning of this chapter, use the information in these sections to complete this table, showing the extent to which the First Five-Year Plan dealt with the problems it was designed to solve.

	Successes	Failures
Economic aims		
Ideological aims		
Political aims		

Social mobility

The First Five-Year Plan was a time of tremendous social mobility. The urban population trebled as peasants moved to the cities to take unskilled jobs in Soviet industry. Existing members of the working class were also promoted. Many became managers of the new Soviet industries, or were retrained as engineers or administrators. Education was reformed to serve the needs of the Five-Year Plan. Workers were encouraged to attend classes in technical subjects, and universities were made accessible to people with minimal academic qualifications. The Soviet Government introduced a programme of 'proletarian advancement' which removed existing 'bourgeois specialists' and replaced them with 150,000 newly trained working-class 'red specialists'.

Production (millions of tonnes)

	1913	1928	1932
Iron	4.2	3.3	6.2
Steel	4.0	4.0	5.9
Coal	29.1	35.4	64.3
Oil	9.2	11.7	21.4

Failures of the First Five-Year Plan

Stalin used the impressive statistics of increased production in heavy industry as evidence of his wise leadership and the triumph of socialism in Russia. Nonetheless, behind Soviet propaganda lay a chaotic economy in which the struggle to meet targets created enormous inefficiencies and low labour productivity.

Meeting targets

Although production had increased, many of the official targets were never met. However, large-scale fraud on the part of local administrators allowed Stalin to claim that the Plan had been 'over-fulfilled'. Local Party officials who failed to meet their production targets were demoted, sacked, or in some cases put on trial and executed as enemies of the state. Under enormous pressure, many local administrators lied about the amount of raw materials that they had been able to produce, creating the impression that targets had been exceeded. Nonetheless, in reality, few production targets were actually achieved (see table).

Targets and actual production (millions of tonnes)

	Target	Production by 1932
Iron	8.0	6.2
Steel	8.3	5.9
Coal	68.0	64.3
Oil	19.0	21.4

Centrally created targets also caused problems in production. Because the targets related only to the quantity of production, local administrators were unconcerned about the quality of their work. Consequently, a large proportion of the materials produced were of such low quality that they were effectively useless. Additionally, as the focus was on production rather than consumption, often the raw materials that were produced were never used and were allowed to decay.

Living and working under the First Five-Year Plan

Improving living standards was never an objective of the Plan, so to some extent the decline of living standards cannot be judged a failure. Nonetheless, it does indicate that the Plan itself was poorly formulated. Workers were sustained by rations which provided a diet significantly poorer than that available under the NEP. Consumer goods virtually disappeared, and queuing became a feature of life in Stalin's society. Additionally, Stalin introduced a seven-day working week, which meant that Sunday – traditionally considered a day of rest – became just another working day.

Working conditions also deteriorated under the first Five-Year Plan. Peasants who had only recently moved to the towns had little experience of industrial work and many perished in the hastily constructed factories. Miners were allowed to work in unsafe conditions because their managers were more concerned about meeting government production targets than they were about safety standards. Labour discipline was harsh. Lateness was criminalised, strikes were outlawed and workers who broke machinery were accused of being capitalist saboteurs and exiled to forced-labour camps. The enormous pressure, however, was counter-productive, and absenteeism and low productivity increased during the Plan.

Many of the workers who built Soviet industry during the First Five-Year Plan were prisoners who were forced to work. These workers, who were known by prison guards as 'white coal', had no rights and were frequently allowed to starve or freeze to death.

The abolition of the free market

One of Stalin's stated aims was to abolish the **free market** and replace it with a centrally planned economy. As already noted, the first Five-Year Plan was too chaotic and imprecise to be described as a plan. It also failed in a second sense as it was unable to destroy the free market. Indeed, in some senses, the nature of the Plan encouraged the formation of a black market. The shortage of consumer goods increased their value and therefore encouraged an illegal trade in products such as vodka, cigarettes, footwear and food. The **black market** was so widespread that it was impossible to police effectively. The Soviet authorities attempted to stamp it out by making an example of those they caught. '**Speculators**' were the subject of **show trials** which usually ended in their exile to forced-labour camps.

Case study: Magnitogorsk

In many ways, the city of Magnitogorsk represents the best and worst of the First Five-Year Plan. Stalin's planners aimed to build a steelworks – and an entire city – from scratch, in an uninhabited part of Russia that was rich in iron ore. A quarter of a million workers were transported to the 'magnetic mountain' and instructed to create Russia's largest steel factory. In 1929, planners commissioned a radical German architect to design a utopian city where workers would be housed in clean, modern accommodation. Thousands of '**shock workers**' volunteered to take part in the visionary project.

The contrast between the vision and the reality was stark. When workers arrived they discovered that few houses were actually built. The majority of workers lived in mud huts, wooden shacks and tents, with no heating or sanitation. Indeed, as late as 1932, construction of the workers' accommodation was still pending. Conditions were so hard that on average, workers left Magnitogorsk to find new work after eighty-two days.

Nonetheless, the 40,000 prison workers and a hard core of dedicated volunteers miraculously turned deserted grasslands into one of Russia's major industrial centres. Some workers were so dedicated that they worked double shifts, and even through the night, in order to create a modern industrial miracle.

The vision of Magnitogorsk was to build a modern industrial society in which workers lived and worked as part of an ideal community. However, in reality, the ideal community was never constructed, and the steelworks was created largely by the slave labour of Stalin's political prisoners.

Conclusion

The First Five-Year Plan was an exercise in 'gigantomania'. Historian Sheila Fitzpatrick describes 'gigantomania' as the worship of size for its own sake. Giant factories were constructed, enormous targets were set and vast quantities of raw materials were produced. However, the focus on scale meant that much of what was produced was unusable. Ambitious targets were increased to the extent that they became fantasies which bore no relation to reality. What is more, record production was accompanied by a decline in living standards and further restrictions in personal freedom. Ultimately, Stalin's 'gigantomania' led to the sacrifice of a generation of Soviet workers in the pursuit of ever-growing, but meaningless, production.

Glossary:

Free market

An economic term which describes a specific type of economic organisation. In a free market, citizens are free to compete against each other as purchasers and providers of goods and services. The government plays an extremely limited role, and therefore production, consumption and prices are determined by the needs of the consumers.

Black market

Similar to a free market, but trading of the goods and services available on the black market is illegal. Consequently, trading of this kind is kept secret.

Show trial

An event in which people are publicly shamed for allegedly criminal acts. The purpose of show trials is to make an example of the 'criminals', in order to persuade the public that similar activity should be avoided.

Speculator

Someone who makes money by buying and selling, rather than producing, goods. Communists believed that speculation was an essentially capitalist activity which exploited those who produced goods.

Shock workers

Volunteers who are sent to work on projects for short periods of time in order to speed up their completion.

Activity: This house believes ...

Historians have disagreed over the extent to which the First Five-Year Plan can be termed a success. Your task is to divide into two teams and formally debate this issue. The first team must propose the motion: 'This house believes that the First Five-Year Plan was an extraordinary success for Russia's economy and people.' The second team must oppose this motion.

Spend some time preparing for this debate. Use the information in this chapter to find general points and specific examples to support your argument.

Each team should appoint a leader. With the help of the team, the team leader should prepare a 5-minute speech, outlining the team's argument. An impartial Chair should also be appointed to oversee the debate and award points.

The structure of the debate

1. The two teams should face each other, with the team leaders in central positions.

2. The Chair should introduce the debate and welcome the teams. The Chair should then invite the team leaders to present their speeches, proposing and opposing the motion.

3. Following the speeches, the floor is opened for contributions (in the form of questions or comments) from the other members of the teams.

4. Points are awarded by the Chair, using the following system:

    - 1 point for each relevant question

    - 2 points for each general statement

    - 5 points for each general statement supported by a specific example.

5. It is the role of the Chair to ensure that politeness is maintained at all times.

6. At the end of the debate, the team with more points is declared the winner.

Taking it further

During the First Five-Year Plan, a number of groups were attacked by the government for causing Russia's economic woes. This 1929 poster, entitled 'Enemies of the Five-Year Plan', depicts eight sections of Russian society who were accused of contributing to Russia's economic backwardness. The groups shown in the poster are: (top row, left to right) landlords, kulaks, journalists, capitalists and (bottom row, left to right) drunkards, priests, Mensheviks, Tsarists. For each of these groups, suggest reasons why the Communists believed they had held back the Russian economy.

1929 poster entitled 'Enemies of the Five-Year Plan'

Chapter 7 Shifting priorities – the Second and Third Five-Year Plans

Key questions

- Why did Stalin introduce the Second and Third Five-Year Plans?
- What were the priorities and key features of the Second and Third Five-Year Plans?
- How far did these Plans meet Stalin's aims?

In 1935, Stalin attended the first All-Russian Conference of Stakhanovites. Surrounded by happy workers, he uttered the immortal words 'life has become better, and happier too'. Stalin's words were so inspiring that they soon became the basis of a popular song, entitled *Song about Stalin*. In the song, the people of Russia promise:

> We will build happiness with unyielding will,
> The road has been shown us by the Leader.
> Having raised red banners high,
> We will follow Stalin to Communism.

In the words of lyricist Alexei Surkov, Stalin 'lives for the happiness of the people', and 'his powerful genius, like a ray of light, illuminates the road to Communism'.

However, according to statistics issued by Gosplan, life was significantly worse under Stalin. In 1937, the diet of Russian workers was worse than it had been ten years previously, during the last years of the NEP. Additionally, labour discipline in Russia's new factories was increasingly harsh. Nonetheless, as this song reflects, many workers felt that the hardships they endured under the Second and Third Five-Year Plans were essential for building socialism in Russia, and defending the Revolution from capitalist enemies abroad.

The Second Five-Year Plan

The Second Five-Year Plan, introduced in 1933, differed considerably from the First. Production targets were more realistic and there was a greater attempt to develop the economy in a more rounded way. Generally, there was some attempt to learn from the problems of the First Five-Year Plan and to develop the economy more effectively.

The priorities of the first three Five-Year Plans

First Five-Year Plan	Second Five-Year Plan	Third Five-Year Plan
1928–1932	1933–1938	1938–1941
• Heavy industry	• Heavy industry • Communications • Electricity • New industries • Consumer goods	• Heavy industry • Rearmament • Creation of a war economy

The priorities of the Second Five-Year Plan

The Second Five-Year Plan, like the First, evolved during its lifetime. Initially, Stalin promised the workers that their standard of living would improve. However, famine in the countryside meant that rationing continued until 1934. From 1934 to 1936, a more concerted effort was made to improve living standards. This changed again in response to German rearmament, and towards the end of the Second Five-Year Plan, military spending replaced any focus on consumer goods.

The Second Five-Year Plan continued to focus on heavy industry. However, the new plan was concerned with consolidating the gains made under the First Five-Year Plan rather than continuing its break-neck pace. Planners also tried to stimulate the growth of new industries, such as chemical processing, and the development of new materials, as well as improving Russia's transport system. In addition, there was recognition that labour productivity was low. To reverse this, the Soviet authorities devised an incentives scheme as well as enforcing a new code of practice which set high expectations of labour performance.

Reasons for changing priorities

Senior figures in Soviet government were aware of the many shortcomings of the First Five-Year Plan. From 1932, a moderate group of Party leaders, unofficially led by Sergei Kirov, argued for a change of focus from within the Politburo. These moderates argued for a better standard of living for the industrial workers. A second shortcoming of the First Five-Year Plan was the inability to transport the vast quantities of raw materials produced. Consequently, improving the transport infrastructure was a new priority for Soviet economic planners.

The moderates also argued for a more conciliatory approach to Russia's peasants. The threat of war, they claimed, had increased following Hitler's election as German Chancellor – and peasant support would be crucial if the Soviet Union went to war. Politburo moderates therefore argued that the government should attempt to win over peasant support by reforming the collective farms and moderating the anti-kulak policy.

Following Kirov's murder at the end of 1934, the moderates lost some of their influence. With the onset of the purges in 1936, the remaining moderates, such as Kuibyshev and Ordzhonikidze, were either arrested and executed or remained quiet. The final revision of the Second Five-Year Plan was also in response to the threat of war. In the absence of moderate opposition, Stalin revised the Plan again, diverting funds from the production of consumer goods to investment in Russia's military resources. Stalin claimed this was justified because of the threat posed by Hitler and Nazi Germany.

The Stakhanovite movement

The First Five-Year Plan revealed weaknesses in Russia's labour force. Productivity and discipline in factories was low and this held back economic growth. The government's solution was to launch a new propaganda campaign appealing to the heroic instincts of Soviet workers whilst at the same time offering real incentives for workers who exceeded their production quotas. In so doing, the Soviet government created a media

legend – Alexei Stakhanov. According to the Soviet media, in August 1935, Stakhanov, a worker in the Donetz Basin coal region, mined 102 tonnes of coal in six hours. This was fourteen times the output of a normal miner. A month later, he exceeded this record, mining 227 tons of coal in a single shift. Stakhanov became an international celebrity, appearing on the cover of the December 1935 edition of *Time* magazine. Stakhanov was rewarded with 200 roubles (approximately one month's wages), a new apartment with a telephone, and tickets to cinemas, clubs and holiday resorts.

Stakhanov was held up as an example to all Russian workers. The message of Soviet propaganda was simple – work hard and you will be rewarded. Compulsory meetings were organised at which workers were encouraged to emulate Stakhanov, and industrial bosses kept records of production totals. In addition, factory bosses were required to reorganise production techniques in order to facilitate increased output. Workers who exceeded their targets were rewarded with better living conditions and financial bonuses.

Stakhanov's achievement was no accident. It was deliberately planned as part of the Second Five-Year Plan's emphasis on labour productivity. He was provided with state-of-the-art equipment and a number of assistants in order to achieve his production 'miracle'. Nonetheless, Stakhanov's legend inspired workers across the USSR and in so doing increased the pace of production during the Second Five-Year Plan.

Alexei Stakhanov, a manufactured 'celebrity' in 1935

Activity: Stakhanovite pylons

Stakhanov was praised for his ability to produce more coal than any other worker in his mine. This brief activity demonstrates the link between competition, reward and increased output. First, produce multiple copies of this picture of a pylon, so that all students have plenty.

Round 1 – all students working individually

- In five minutes, colour in as many of the pictures as possible, using at least five different colours for each pylon.

Round 2 – divided into three teams

- In five minutes, each team must colour in as many of the pictures as possible, using at least five different colours for each pylon.

- Teams should have the same resources.

- Teams must organise themselves as efficiently as possible.

- The team that produces the largest number of finished pylons wins!

Round 3 – reorganise and try again

- Repeat Round 2.

- Teams must try to beat the total of the winning team from Round 2.

- Teams may reorganise themselves in order to increase their efficiency.

1. Why did output increase in Round 2 and Round 3?

2. What incentives were there to reorganise production more efficiently after Round 2?

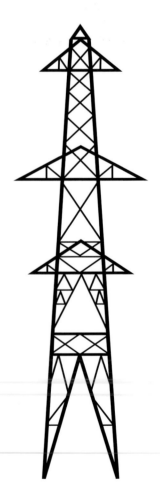

Source 7.1: A female worker describes her working day at the Dnieper Hydroelectric Power Station

We were working on Section 34. I was sending up concrete, 95 tubs that day. We raised the tub. The concrete was stamped down. Suddenly I saw some tar paper fall into it. I went to get it, then started back. The board under me began to sink, and I was dragged down. I grabbed hold of the ladder, but my hand was slipping. Everybody got scared, one of the girls screamed. Another ran over to me, grabbed hold of my hand and dragged me out. I was full of concrete … the tar singed my arms. I went to dry off and then went straight back to work. I worked the full shift.

Transcribed from the 1934 Soviet film, *Three Songs About Lenin*

Achievements of the Second Five-Year Plan

The targets for the Second Five-Year Plan were more realistic than the First, and its achievements were more modest. Overall, the government claimed that the Second Five-Year Plan had been 'over-fulfilled' by 3%. The production of raw materials continued to expand. The output of steel, for example, trebled, largely due to production from the new plants such as Magnitogorsk.

Transport, one of the new priorities of the Plan, could also boast some successes. The first lines of the Moscow metro were opened in 1935. Additionally, the Moscow–Volga Canal was completed between 1932 and 1937. The canal allowed the transportation of large quantities of material throughout western Russia.

In terms of living standards, the pressure of the Politburo moderates resulted in some limited successes. In early 1934, bread rationing was ended. This was soon followed by the end of the rationing of other commodities such as meat and butter. The wages of industrial workers also increased in real terms. The improvement of living standards was the result of small, but important, reforms in agriculture. Moderates in the Politburo argued that peasants should be allowed small plots of land to farm privately. This policy was adopted in 1934, and as a result Russia was able to recover fairly quickly following the famines of the previous years.

Finally, in response to fears of an imminent war with Germany, defence spending rose from 4 per cent of total government expenditure in 1933 to 17 per cent in 1937. Notably, the new focus on defence came at the expense of living standards.

Problems with the Second Five-Year Plan

The Second Five-Year Plan, like the First, suffered from a number of chronic problems. First, although the economy was supposedly planned, in practice, there was little coordination between the different branches of industry. For example, in order to meet their targets, factory managers would hoard resources that were in short supply. This created even greater scarcity of resources. Another example of the poor coordination was the lack of spare parts experienced in many industries. Without the appropriate parts, broken machinery remained idle and unproductive. Secondly, fear of execution or exile meant that nobody was prepared to criticise the Plan, report errors, or suggest that targets were unattainable. Consequently, the practice of lying about figures that emerged under the First Five-Year Plan continued into the Second.

Despite some increase in the standard of living between 1934 and 1936, shortages of essential items remained a daily reality for Russia's citizens. A diary entry from 1934 describes the poverty: 'the most anyone can dream of is to own two or three sets of clothes, a bicycle, and the opportunity to buy grapes at 11 roubles a kilogram'. Historian Sheila Fitzpatrick argues that during the 1930s shopping was 'a survival skill'. Wise housewives would buy any consumer goods that were available – whether they needed them or not – in order to trade them at a later date. The availability of shoes, to

take an everyday example, was problematic throughout the 1930s. In 1931, the government outlawed the private production of shoes because of the shortage of leather. Consequently, consumers had to rely on state-produced shoes which were of such low quality that they sometimes fell apart on the day they were bought. Shoe shortages were so extreme that in 1934, a queue of 6,000 people waited for more than a day outside the one shoe shop in central Leningrad. When the shop opened, police were called to avoid a riot.

Housing and amenities, already a problem during the First Five-Year Plan, failed to improve. For example, there was not a single bathhouse for the 650,000 people in the Liubertsy district of Moscow. Indeed, many of the new houses completed during the Second Five-Year Plan were built without running water or sewerage.

Finally, the mid-1930s saw the emergence of new and sometimes stark social inequalities. First, at the beginning of the Second Five-Year Plan, Stalin explicitly stated that socialism did not entail wage equality. He argued that every society must provide incentives for hard work, and therefore inequality was an essential part of the new Soviet system. The emphasis on incentives was clear in the Stakhanovite movement, where the most productive workers would be rewarded with opulent flats and access to luxury food. A second source of inequality was the privileges enjoyed by members of the Communist Party. The 55,000 senior Communists were entitled to better food, better clothes and better accommodation than the average citizen, due to their seniority within the Communist Party. For example, Stalin's new elite were entitled to chauffeur-driven limousines, private houses and holiday homes, and in some cases reserved seats in cinemas and at the opera. Communist Party officials also had access to 'secret shops' which contained consumer goods unavailable to the general public. However, most Party members were still worse off than the average worker in Britain or America at that time.

The Third Five-Year Plan

The Third Five-Year Plan ended abruptly after just three and a half years, because of Russia's entry into the Second World War. In many ways, this Plan was devised to prepare Russia for war with Germany. Broadly, the Third Five-Year Plan applied the methods developed during the First Five-Year Plan to war production. Thus, while the total quantity of military goods increased significantly, there were ongoing problems with production methods and the quality of the goods produced.

Rearmament

The Third Five-Year Plan continued the rearmament which had begun during the final phase of the Second Five-Year Plan. By 1940, a third of government investment went to the armed forces, doubling the proportion since 1937. Once again, planners diverted resources away from consumer goods in order to release funds for defence spending.

The Third Five-Year Plan initiated a number of important innovations in Soviet military technology. For example, in 1939, Gosplan ordered the construction of nine new aircraft factories. Stalin oversaw the work

Source 7.2: From the memoirs of Oksana Makhnach, the daughter of two Soviet cinematographers. Writing in 1981, she recalls the impoverished living conditions of her childhood.

The floorboards were painted red because there was no carpet. … Today's young people, who live for material possessions, would think that they were visiting a store of discarded furniture or even a rubbish dump. All our kitchen goods were stored in a home-made cupboard. I slept on a fold-up camp-bed, behind the china cupboard in a corner of the living room.

Taken from: *The Whisperers: Private Life in Stalin's Russia* by Orlando Figes (2007)

Take note

1. As you work through this section, make a table with the priorities of the Plan in one column, and the rationale behind these priorities in another.
2. List the successes and failures of the Third Five-Year Plan in terms of:
   • Rearmament
   • Heavy industry
   • Worker discipline.

personally and reviewed figures on the number of aeroplanes and engines built on a daily basis. However, as in the First Five-Year Plan, while production rose, much of what was produced was unusable.

In May 1941, Stalin received secret intelligence that the German army now had eight million men, 12,000 tanks, 52,000 guns and 20,000 aircraft. Believing that war was imminent, Stalin took direct control of the defence industry. Additionally, the Central Committee decreed that all of the country's resources should be mobilised in preparation for war. To some extent, Stalin's intervention in rearmament ended Gosplan's responsibility for Russia's military economy, and therefore between May and June 1941, the Third Five-Year Plan came to a premature end.

Heavy industry

Once again, heavy industry formed the backbone of the Plan. Coal production leapt from 128 million tonnes in 1937 to 166 million tonnes in 1940. However, the production of crude oil rose only marginally (from 29 million tonnes in 1937 to 31 million tonnes in 1940) and the production of steel stagnated.

Worker discipline

Building on the measures introduced in the Second Five-Year Plan to boost labour productivity, the Third Five-Year Plan introduced harsh new measures to ensure labour discipline. The First and Second Five-Year Plans had resulted in enormous social upheaval. Peasants left the countryside to work in the new factories and workers were promoted into management or administrative positions. In the atmosphere of rapid social advancement, many Russians regularly switched jobs in search of better pay and conditions. Moshe Lewin describes this as a 'quicksand society' due to the rapidly shifting patterns of employment. This rapid flux created problems for Soviet industry because factories could not guarantee that they would be able to recruit or retain labour. This problem was addressed with the introduction of 'internal passports' in 1940. These restricted the ability of workers to move from job to job, and therefore ensured that factories were guaranteed a stable supply of labour.

In the countryside too, the government attempted to reassert its control over peasant farmers. According to a Politburo report, commissioned in May 1939, agricultural production was to be boosted by limiting the amount of time that peasants were allowed to devote to their private land. The report also proposed reducing the size of private plots. Both of these measures were an attempt to refocus the energies of Russia's peasants on production for state collective farms.

Problems in the implementation of the Third Five-Year Plan

The administration of the Third Five-Year Plan was complicated by Stalin's purges which created chaos in Gosplan, as well as across Russian industry more generally. The purges resulted in the removal and execution of many experienced industrial managers, leading to a return to the planning chaos that had characterised the First Five-Year Plan.

Further problems were created by the removal of the moderate group within the Politburo in 1936. Moderates such as Kirov had been able to offer creative solutions which led to improved productivity and helped consolidate the achievements of the First Five-Year Plan. In their absence, the inefficiencies of the Third Five-Year Plan continued unchallenged, and Stalin reverted to terror in order to motivate managers and workers to meet their targets.

Conclusion: Russia in 1941

Between 1928 and 1941, Russia was transformed from a semi-capitalist rural society to a highly industrialised, urbanised society. Stalin's objective had been to fortify Russia and to turn her into a world power. In both of these senses, he succeeded. Nonetheless, industrialisation was highly problematic. First, the Five-Year Plans consistently over-emphasised heavy industry and under-invested in consumer goods. Politburo moderates were briefly able to shift the focus of the Second Five-Year Plan, and living conditions improved as a result. This brief respite – from the beginning of 1934 to the end of 1936 – is often referred to as the 'three good years'. However, for the majority of the 1928 to 1941 period, everyday life in Soviet Russia was dominated by hard work and chronic shortages. Secondly, Stalin never fulfilled his aim of increasing labour productivity. The Stakhanovite movement motivated some workers to produce more, but in general, workers remained poorly motivated and continued to produce at the rate that they had done during the First Five-Year Plan. Consequently, while large amounts of raw materials were produced, and industry grew at a prodigious rate, the Russian economy as a whole remained hopelessly inefficient.

Activity: Failing to plan is planning to fail!

1. Using the information in this and the previous chapter, copy and complete the following summary table:

	Priorities	Successes	Failures
First Five-Year Plan			
Second Five-Year Plan			
Third Five-Year Plan			

2. Draw a timeline of the years 1928–1941, marking on it the three Five-Year Plans. Above the timeline, record the key priorities of each Plan. For the Second Five-Year Plan, there is a series of priorities, and these should be marked on the timeline in chronological order. Below the timeline, explain the reasons why Stalin adopted these priorities.

3. How far do you agree that the changing priorities of the Five-Year Plans suggest that Stalin had no overall scheme for Soviet economic policy, but was merely responding to events?

Taking it further

In a Politburo meeting of 1928, Rykov shouted at Stalin 'Your policy does not even smell of economics!' In saying this, Rykov was suggesting that Stalin had political motives for introducing the Five-Year Plans, rather than economic ones. How far do you agree that the Five-Year Plans were primarily designed to consolidate Stalin's power?

Chapter 8 The 'Great Retreat' – women, family and education in Stalin's Russia

Key questions

- In what ways did education and family life change from the 1920s to the 1930s?
- What was the link between educational reform and the Five-Year Plans?
- How far did the opportunities available to women change under Stalin?

In 1936, Stalin announced that the Soviet people were the first in history to live free from exploitation. Stalin based this claim on the fact that collectivisation and the Five-Year Plans had expelled capitalism from Russia. Sadly, Stalin's analysis of Russian society was highly simplistic, for it overlooked any exploitation that was not related to class. Within Stalin's 'classless society', there were still inequalities – specifically, between men and women. Women were still expected to provide unpaid childcare, to run the home, and to bear the brunt of educating children. What is more, this inequality of opportunity became more pronounced as part of a deliberate policy of Stalin's government.

Take note

As you work through this section, copy and complete the following table:

Evidence that women had greater opportunities in Stalinist Russia	Evidence that women had limited opportunities in Stalinist Russia

Women

In the 1930s, Zhenotdel, a women's branch of the Communist Central Committee, was closed down due to the fact that the Communist Party believed that sexual equality had been achieved. However, the assumption that women and men were now equal reflected how little attention senior male members of the Communist Party paid to the role of women. During the 1930s, many women entered the Russian workforce for the first time. Nonetheless, the Communist Party reasserted traditional gender roles.

Making money

Women joined the industrial labour force in large numbers because of the demands of the Five-Year Plans. In 1928, at the beginning of the First Five-Year Plan, only 3 million women were employed in Russia's industry. This leapt to over 13 million by 1940. By 1940, 41 per cent of workers in heavy industry were women, and in some cities, such as Leningrad, women accounted for almost half of industrial workers. The Soviet authorities recognised the important contribution made by women to Russian industry and therefore increased the allocation of places in higher or technical education available to women, from 20 per cent in 1929 to 40 per cent in 1940. Nonetheless, the Soviet authorities continued to pay women less than their male counterparts. Indeed, throughout this period, the income of women was only 60–65 per cent of the income of men doing the same job.

Women were also important in the agricultural economy. By 1945, 80 per cent of collective farm workers were women. Additionally, women were represented in the Stakhanovite movement in the countryside. The most celebrated rural Stakhanovites were both female. Pasha Angelina gained

national fame as the organiser of the first Women's Tractor Brigade. In 1936 Maria Demchanko was also the subject of a great deal of publicity due to her pledge to harvest four times the average yield of sugar beet. In the same year, 62 per cent of delegates from cattle and dairy farms to the Stakhanovite Livestock Workers' Conference were milkmaids.

Making babies

The trauma of industrialisation and collectivisation led to a dramatic decline in the birth rate in the early 1930s, and the Communist government introduced policies to try to reverse this trend. First, rewards were introduced for mothers who had large families. Women who had more than six children qualified for state help. The rewards on offer were considerable. Mothers with seven children received 2,000 roubles a year for five years. This figure rose to 5,000 roubles for mothers with eleven children. Immediately after the law was passed the government proclaimed it a success. The Moscow registry office, for example, received four thousand applications for support within the first month of the new policy – 2,730 from families with eight children, 1,032 from families with ten children, and 160 from families with more than ten children.

In 1936, the Soviet authorities also discouraged abortion, making it all but illegal. The new law banned terminations except where they were necessary to save the life of a pregnant woman. Doctors who performed abortions on 'undeserving' women could be sentenced to two years imprisonment. Husbands who put pressure on their wives to terminate a pregnancy would face the same penalty.

Making homes

In addition to working on collective farms or in Soviet industry, women were expected to be responsible for household chores, such as cooking, cleaning and childcare. Indeed, although men had been liberated from their domestic duties, such as chopping wood and carrying water, due to mechanisation, women had none of these advantages. On average, they spent five times longer on domestic responsibilities than men.

Wives of Party officials were expected not to work, but to devote themselves to managing 'a well-ordered Communist home'. At the end of the 1920s, it was common for Communist families to employ nannies in order that Communist Party wives could still be involved in political work. However, by the mid-1930s, this practice was frowned upon and female members of the Communist Party were encouraged to do their duty at home.

Wifes of Party officials were also expected to be involved in the 'wife activists' movement'. This attempted to create solidarity between women who were devoted to being 'mistresses of the great Soviet home'. The movement organised nurseries and activities for seriously ill children, setting up schools and libraries, and supervised factory canteens, as well as charitable work. For example, the wives of senior officials at Magnitogorsk organised a masked ball, the proceeds of which were distributed to the needy. Broadly, the 'wife activists' were attempting to 'mother' the whole of Soviet society. However, members of the wives' movement were also expected to be ideal mothers

Take note

As you work through this section, answer these questions:

1. What is meant by the 'Great Retreat'?
2. In what ways did Soviet propaganda promote Soviet family policy?
3. Why did the Soviet authorities seek to promote marriage?
4. In what ways did the Soviet authorities attempt to encourage marriage and discourage divorce?

and partners. Their homes were to be 'examples of order, warmth and feminine comfort', and their husbands were to expect members of the wives' movement to be caring and attentive.

Family life

The 1930s marked a turning point in the Communist understanding of the family. In the first phase of the revolution, Communists had proclaimed that the family and marriage were 'bourgeois institutions'. This attitude was reflected by various experiments in communal living and free love which were intended to 'take the old family by storm' – to replace the traditional family with a new Communist lifestyle. By contrast, the mid-1930s were described as the 'Great Retreat', where traditional gender roles and sexual attitudes were reasserted across Russia.

Propaganda

In Stalin's Russia, the family was seen as the 'primary cell of our society'. Indeed, the family became the Soviet government's favourite metaphor for describing itself and its people. The working class were described as 'one big family'. Stalin was portrayed as 'the father of the Soviet people'. In 1935, for the first time, the Soviet press started a campaign to show Stalin as a family man. In October, Stalin made a highly publicised visit to his mother in Tblisi. Soon after, Soviet magazines published the first photographs of Stalin and his children. Stalin's faithfulness to his wife, whose suicide in 1932 was omitted from Soviet propaganda, was held up as an example which all Communists were expected to follow.

Propaganda in the second half of the 1930s stressed that men were undermining the family. Posters and films showed them as responsible for family break-up, the neglect of children and for abandoning their wives. Women, on the other hand, were described as responsible, noble, self-sacrificing and the essential source of strength at the heart of the family. The aim of Soviet propaganda was to stress the importance of family and stigmatise the irresponsible men who were the cause of so much family break-up.

Marriage

The value of marriage was re-emphasised by the Stalinist government during the 1930s. Indeed, the government took several steps to reintroduce romance and glamour to the institution of marriage. For example, wedding rings – banned in 1928 – were reintroduced in 1936. Secondly, in the same year, the administration started printing marriage certificates on high quality paper to symbolise the importance of the union. Party members who were married were given more spacious accommodation and their own dacha (holiday home in the country), and were encouraged to take family holidays in Party holiday resorts.

Communist husbands were expected to be the main income earners in the family. They were also expected to be devoted to their families and could be expelled from the Party for having affairs.

The results of Soviet propaganda promoting marriage were impressive. The

1937 census showed that 91 per cent of men and 82 per cent of women aged between 30 and 39 were married.

Sex under Stalin

Following the 1917 Revolution, many within the Bolshevik Party looked forward to a new era of sexual freedom. In practice, however, free love led to divorce and family breakdown. Consequently, Stalin reintroduced a more traditional perspective on sexual morality. In 1934, the government launched a campaign aimed at young people promoting sexual abstinence. This was backed up by police action against young women who had an 'immoral appearance'. Collective farm chairmen also attempted to support the new initiative by ordering 'medical virginity checks' on young women. Finally, incest, bigamy, adultery and male homosexuality, which had been legalised in 1930, were re-criminalised in 1936. For example, A.V. Malodetkin, an industrial worker in Moscow, was sentenced in 1936 to two years imprisonment for being married to four different women, three at his factory and one in his village. Malodetkin's only defence was that he had married four times because he 'had nothing better to do'.

Soviet policy makers also turned against contraception. Under the Five-Year Plans, Gosplan assigned no resources to the production of contraception aids. Consequently, contraceptive devices all but disappeared during the 1930s. The Soviet state consolidated this move in 1936 in a secret directive that officially ended the sale of all birth-control resources.

Divorce and family break-up

The Communist experiments with free love and relaxed divorce laws during the 1920s had resulted in spiralling divorce rates. By 1927, in urban areas such as Moscow, two-thirds of all marriages ended in divorce. The picture was little better in the countryside, where the divorce rate was 50 per cent. The rising divorce rate led to horrendous social problems. As marriages broke down, families split up, the number of orphans increased and women were impoverished.

In many cases the state was responsible for dealing with these problems, and in the mid-1930s it took steps to stem the rising tide of family break-up by limiting the availability of divorce. In June 1936, new divorce laws were passed which made divorce a more complex and expensive process. The cost of a divorce was 50 roubles (one week's wages) in the first case, 150 for a second divorce, and 300 roubles for any subsequent divorce. Additionally, men were expected to pay one-third of their earnings to support their child, or 60 per cent if they had left three or more children. The penalty for failing to meet these obligations was two years in prison.

In addition to passing laws, the Communist Party took a variety of steps to prevent family break-up. Indeed, women who could get no help from Russia's courts turned to local Party bosses. Some local Parties were prepared to track down absconding husbands and force them to make regular payments to help support their ex-wives and children. The Siberian Communist Party went further, organising a conference of young women who were encouraged to discuss the ways in which their lives had been ruined by men. The Soviet

Source 8.1: *Pravda* editorial on new divorce and abortion laws, June 1936

When we speak of strengthening the Soviet family, we are speaking precisely of the struggle against bourgeois attitudes towards marriage, women and the family. So-called 'free love' and all disorderly sex life are bourgeois through and through, and have nothing to do with socialist principles. The elite of our country are excellent family men, who dearly love their children. And the man who does not take care of his marriage and abandons his children is also a bad worker and a poor member of society.

Source 8.2: Decree on the Teaching of Civic History, May 1934

The Council of People's Commissars of the USSR and the Central Committee of the All-Union Communist Party find that the teaching of History in schools is unsatisfactory. Textbooks and instruction are too abstract. Instead of teaching in a lively, engaging form, with a focus on important events, chronology, and the characters of historical people, pupils are presented with abstract definitions.

Glossary: Komsomol

The Communist Union of Youth. It was created in 1922 and catered for young people from the ages of 14 to 28.

Take note

Soviet education in the 1930s was heavily influenced by the needs of the Five-Year Plans. As you work through this section, make a bullet-pointed list of the ways in which education was reformed to aid Russia's economic development.

press also played its part in hounding men who had deserted their wives. For example, the trade union newspaper *Trud* reported a story of a bank manager who moved from city to city in order to evade his responsibilities. According to *Trud*, the manager had abandoned himself to a life of 'wildness, degeneracy and baseness'. Clearly, there was some official support for women, but it was only available for women who were prepared to conform to the role of wife and mother.

Education under Stalin

Stalin's attitude to education was that discipline, hard work, and tradition should be reasserted. At home, this meant that children were expected to obey their parents, and at school, this was reflected in a new curriculum and an emphasis on conventional teaching methods.

Raising good citizens

During the 1920s, radical Communists had urged children and young people to challenge the bourgeois authority of parents and teachers. Stalin reversed this policy – arguing that discipline was essential for young people. Soviet youth organisations, such as the **Komsomol**, reinforced this message in their publications. *Komsomolskaia Pravda,* for example, instructed children to 'respect and love your parents, even if they are old-fashioned and do not like the Komsomol'. Pavlik Morozov became the Soviet government's example of a perfect child. Pavlik, who was supposedly killed by a kulak at the age of fourteen, was described as a hard-working and obedient school child, an example for others to follow.

Parents were expected to teach their children to respect the Soviet government and to enthusiastically embrace their duties as Soviet citizens. According to one Soviet educationalist, writing in 1935, 'the family's duties in child-rearing are based on its obligation to cultivate good citizens'.

Formal education

Russian education in the 1920s stressed Communist ideals. In August 1931, however, the Central Committee attacked Soviet education for neglecting literacy and numeracy. To rectify this, a new curriculum was introduced in 1935, along with a series of textbooks. The teaching of History is a good example of the change that Stalin brought to education. During the 1920s, History was taught in terms of class struggle. However, under Stalin, the history of social classes was rejected and replaced with the histories of great Russians, such as Ivan the Terrible and Peter the Great. The teaching of History also became more nationalistic, stressing the history of the Russian nation, rather than the history of the working class.

The 1935 curriculum also set out a series of core subject areas, such as reading, writing, Communist ideology and science that all children were expected to learn. The state specified that homework was to be set regularly, and it introduced national examinations. The curriculum was accompanied by a new emphasis on strict discipline. School discipline was designed to prepare children for the harsh regulation of the workplace under the Five-Year Plans. The spirit of Stakhanov was also extended to teachers.

In 1936, Olga Fedorovna Leonova pledged that all of her students would gain excellent grades. When she met this target, her example of heroic hard work and dedication to Communism was praised across the Russian media. Clearly, both teaching and learning in Russia were influenced by the methods of the Five-Year Plans.

Finally, state spending on education was reduced in order to free up resources for the Five-Year Plans. To make up the short fall, fees were introduced. In practice, the Party and trade unions offered grants and scholarships to help students get through their education. This system favoured the sons and daughters of Communist Party officials and was therefore another incentive for loyal service to the Party.

Conclusion

Stalin's radicalism in agriculture and industry required a more disciplined and ordered society. For this reason, his social policy was considerably more conservative than his economic policy. The aspirations of the October Revolution, such as the liquidation of the bourgeois family, the liberation of women from the home and the reform of education, were replaced by traditional approaches to Russia's social problems. Therefore, the 'Great Retreat' was an essential part of Stalin's revolution from above.

Taking it further

During the 1930s the Party acknowledged that citizens were entitled to a 'personal life'. A 'personal life' was defined as those aspects of a citizen's family life that were expected to serve the Party but in which the Party allowed some personal choice. To what extent, given the pressures of the Five-Year Plans and the laws on marriage, sexuality and divorce, was it possible for Soviet citizens to have a 'personal life'?

Activity: Communist 'Lonely Hearts'

1. Imagine you are a male member of the Russian Communist Party who is in search of a wife.

2. Using the information in this chapter on women and family life, write a 'lonely hearts' advertisement for a Soviet Paper.

3. Your 'lonely hearts' advert should include:

   - A detailed list of the characteristics you are looking for in a future bride

   - What you can offer, given your position in the Communist Party

   - How you envisage your future life together.

4. Aim to write at least 150 words, and include as much specific detail as possible.

Activity: Stalin's speech writer

1. Imagine you are Stalin's speech writer. He intends to make a speech on education for the Seventeenth Congress of the All-Russia Communist Party in 1934.

2. You must write a 200-word speech for him to deliver at this meeting.

3. The speech must outline the ways in which educational policy is to be reformed in order to serve the needs of the Five-Year Plans.

Skills Builder 2: Planning answers to questions on causation and change

Questions on causation

In the AS examination you may be asked questions on causation – questions about what caused historical events to take place.

Some questions may ask you to explain why something happened. For example:

> (A) Why did Stalin launch the First Five-Year Plan?

Other questions on causation will ask you to assess the importance of one cause of an event, in relation to other causes. These often begin with 'How far' or 'To what extent'. Here is an example:

> (B) How far do you agree that Communist ideology was the main reason for the introduction of the First Five-Year Plan?

Planning your answer

Before you write your essay you need to make a plan. In the exam you will have to do this very quickly! The first thing to do is to identify the key points you will make in your answer. Let's look at some examples.

When planning an answer to Question (A) you need to note down reasons why the First Five-Year Plan was introduced. You can do this in the form of a list or a mindmap.

When planning an answer to Question (B) you need to think about the importance of each reason. You could:

- Write a list of all the reasons, then number them in order of importance.

- Draw a mindmap with 'First Five-Year Plan' at the centre, and put the most important reasons near the middle and the least important reasons further away.

It is much easier to assess the importance of one factor when you have a list of all the relevant factors in front of you!

The information you require for these answers can be found in Chapter 6. Go to Chapter 6 and identify the reasons why Stalin introduced the First Five-Year Plan. Focus not only on ideological factors, but on those linked to the economy and to politics as well.

Linking the causes

Once you have identified the relevant information and organised it, it is important to highlight links between the reasons.

In making your plan, try grouping reasons together which have links. If you have produced a list of reasons, you may want to rearrange the points where you can identify clear links between them. If you have drawn a 'mindmap', you could draw arrows between the linked points.

Writing your answer

For Question (A) above, you could write a paragraph on each cause. Alternatively, you might want to start with what you think is the most important cause, and then deal with the other causes.

For Question (B) above, it is essential that you refer to the relative importance of different causes, focusing particularly on the role of ideology. Remember to answer the question! You might want to deal with ideological factors first and then assess the importance of other points for the creation of the First Five-Year Plan. Make sure you write a separate paragraph for each reason that you identify.

Questions about change

These questions will require you to explain how far a specified factor changed during a historical period. Examples of this type of question would be:

> (C) How far did the role of women in Russia change between 1928 and 1941?

> (D) How far did the economic position of industrial workers improve between 1928 and 1941?

Planning your answer

When you plan, organise your material in a way that will help you to answer the question.

For instance, for Question (C) you could begin by listing two or three ways in which the role of women changed in Stalin's Russia. Having done that, you could list two or three ways in which the role of women stayed the same. Alternatively, you could arrange this information on one or two mindmaps. Remember that your answer needs to be balanced. Therefore, it should provide points for and against change.

Each of these points will form the basis for one paragraph in your answer. In the last Skills Builder section, you considered the importance of providing specific examples to support your points. Don't forget this!

When you plan, there is no need to organise your material in a chronological way. This may encourage the writing of descriptive or narrative-style answers. Such answers may contain lots of accurate and relevant historical information, but may not be directly focused on the question.

Writing your answer

In Questions (C) and (D) you are asked 'how far' in relation to changes. So in your final paragraph, the conclusion, you will be expected to *make a judgement*. Based on the historical evidence you have presented in your answer, you should decide, and state, whether you believe the situation mainly changed or stayed the same.

Activity: how much have you learned?

Here are some examples of questions which deal with causation and change. First, identify the causation questions and give a reason to support your choice. Then identify the questions which deal with change and give a reason for your choice. Finally, choose one 'causation' question and one 'change' question and produce a plan for each, showing how you would organise your answer.

> (E) How far did the First Five-Year Plan differ from the Second and Third Five-Year Plans?

> (F) To what extent was Communist ideology the main reason for Stalin's 'Great Retreat'?

> (G) How far was the failure of the NEP the main cause of collectivisation?

> (H) How far did collectivisation improve Russian agriculture in the period 1928–1941?

Chapter 9 Awakening terror – Stalin and Yagoda, 1934–1936

Key questions

- Why did Stalin launch the Great Terror at the end of 1934?
- In what ways did the Great Terror differ from Communist repression before 1934?
- What was the scale of the Great Terror under Stalin and Yagoda?

The Party Congress of February 1934 was declared 'the Congress of Victors'. Delegates from around the USSR came to celebrate the giant achievements of Stalin's industrial policy. Stalin's speech was nothing more than a detailed list of economic statistics – but the Congress responded with a standing ovation. Zinoviev, Kamenev and Bukharin also spoke of their past errors and 'Stalin, the leader of genius'. Everything went according to plan, except for the vote for the Central Committee on the final day of the conference. Unexpectedly, a quarter of the Conference voted against Stalin's re-election to the Central Committee. Conference officials panicked, and the real results were covered up. But from that time on, Stalin viewed every delegate who had attended the Conference as an enemy – and within three years, over a thousand of the Congress's twelve hundred delegates had been executed as part of Stalin's Great Terror. The Congress then became known as 'the Congress of the Damned'.

Timeline

1927	Kirov elected Chairman of Leningrad Party
1932	Riutin expelled from the Party
1934	February: Congress of Victors July: OGPU renamed NKVD (People's Commissariat of Internal Affairs) with Genrikh Yagoda appointed as Head of the NKVD (People's Commissar for Internal Affairs) December: Kirov assassinated: beginning of the Great Terror
1935	January: Zinoviev and Kamenev arrested for conspiracy to murder Kirov

Totalitarianism

During the 1930s, journalists, historians and political scientists began to discuss a new phenomenon that they described as 'totalitarianism'. In essence, totalitarianism describes a form of government in which all areas of life are brought under government control. Totalitarianism is different from traditional dictatorships, such as Tsarism, because it demands enthusiasm and commitment from its citizens, whereas traditional dictatorships merely expect a lack of opposition.

Leninist origins of the police state

Stalin's Russia is one of the clearest examples of totalitarianism. During the 1930s the Soviet government extended its influence over the economy, tightened its censorship and its control of artists, and unleashed a reign of terror against its citizens.

Political terror was an established part of Soviet political life long before Stalin became leader of the Communist Party. Lenin, Trotsky, Bukharin – indeed all Communists – believed it was essential for the survival of the revolutionary regime. Nonetheless, the role of Russia's secret police, the

Take note

Having read this section, write a definition of totalitarianism, using fewer than twenty-five words, if possible.

Cheka, steadily expanded as Stalin's power increased. In the later 1920s, the OGPU, the name by which they were now known, began to be concerned with opposition politicians within the Communist Party. For example, they enforced the house arrest of Zinoviev and Kamenev and spied on Bukharin. But the OGPU did not use physical methods against Communists and were therefore nicknamed 'the dry guillotine' by Party members.

In the first years of Stalin's rule, the role of the OGPU changed again. First, from 1928, they organised dekulakisation. This involved the mass exile of perhaps ten million peasants. Secondly, they organised prison labour camps that contributed to the construction of projects such as Magnitogorsk. Finally, they spied on workers and peasants and organised show trials of so-called saboteurs who had held back production.

Causes of the Great Terror

Historically, the Soviet secret police had stopped short of terrorising the Communist Party. But at the end of 1934 Stalin launched a wave of **political terror** that claimed a million lives and resulted in twelve million people being sent to forced-labour camps. Stalin had a variety of reasons for pursuing such an extreme policy. First, events inside the Communist Party persuaded him that many of his so-called comrades could no longer be trusted. Secondly, Stalin's paranoia was fed by his secretive police system, finally renamed the NKVD. Thirdly, the **purges** were bound up with his economic goals. Finally, the purges allowed Stalin to remove his political rivals.

The Congress of Victors

The 'Congress of Victors' was intended to be a celebration of Stalin's economic achievements. However, the Congress worried Stalin for several reasons. First, when the Congress voted to elect the Central Committee, Kirov rather than Stalin topped the poll. Kirov received 1,225 votes, compared to Stalin's 927 votes. The result indicated that Kirov was more popular within the Communist Party than Stalin. Finally, a group of old Bolsheviks approached Kirov following the vote and tried to persuade him to stand as General Secretary. Although Kirov refused, Stalin quickly found out about the plan. For Stalin, these events were evidence that he had to purge the Party, because it could no longer be trusted.

Paranoia

Stalin's paranoia led to the Great Terror, because he felt unable to trust many within the Communist Party and therefore acted to remove those he saw as potential threats. Although Stalin was the unchallenged ruler of Soviet Russia, he believed that he still had many enemies. Recent history made Stalin anxious. Trotsky, Zinoviev and Bukharin had all held leading positions in the Party, and then fallen from power. It was entirely possible, or so Stalin thought, that he would suffer the same fate. What is more, he distrusted his former rivals and did not believe that they were truly converted to his version of socialism. He was also fearful of old Communists, who had been members of the Party since before the Civil War. They knew the truth about

Taking it further

One of the best known examples of totalitarianism is the fictional regime described in George Orwell's novel *Nineteen Eighty-Four*, which was inspired, in part, by Orwell's knowledge of the terroristic practices of Stalin's Russia. In many ways Orwell's novel captures the essence of a totalitarian society. If you have not yet read it, maybe you should!

Glossary:
Political terror

Term used to describe the violent acts of the government against its people which are designed to discourage and eliminate opposition.

Purge

The process by which a ruling party cleanses itself of unwanted members. Originally, in the USSR, purges were designed to rid the ruling Communist Party of members who had joined for the 'wrong' reasons or who had become corrupt. During the 1920s, members who were purged simply lost their jobs and were expelled from the Party. But under Stalin, the process became more bloody.

Cause of the Great Terror	Specific examples	Explanation – how exactly did this cause the Great Terror?
Congress of Victors		
Paranoia		
Terror economics		
The murder of Kirov		

Sergei Kirov

(1886–1934)

Kirov replaced Zinoviev as Chairman of the Leningrad Communist Party in 1927. In 1928, he sided with Stalin against Bukharin and the Right Opposition. He was a committed supporter of collectivisation and the First Five-Year Plan. However, in early 1934 he became the unofficial leader of a group of moderates within the Politburo. This group had no intention of replacing Stalin. Rather, they attempted to persuade him to modify the aims of the Second Five-Year Plan in order to produce more consumer goods and to adopt a more tolerant attitude to the peasants and Stalin's former political opponents. Kirov was highly popular and one of few senior Communists who was happy to travel around the country unguarded.

his rise to power and Lenin's view that he did not deserve to be General Secretary, let alone leader of Soviet Russia.

Additionally, Stalin feared that the Red Army and the secret police had too much power. His lack of control of these bodies led him to fear assassination attempts. Genrikh Yagoda, who in the early 1930s was second in command of the OGPU, attempted to win Stalin's favour by fuelling his suspicions and therefore deepening his paranoia. The OGPU – and later the NKVD – compiled extensive reports on discontent with collectivisation in the countryside. Yagoda also collected intelligence suggesting that many Communist officials questioned the wisdom of Stalin's policies.

Terror economics

The Great Terror served two important economic functions. First, it allowed Stalin to blame economic problems on political enemies. The ongoing difficulties with the Five-Year Plans could be explained by the presence of 'wreckers' in the workforce. These 'wreckers', according to Stalin, were in the employ of Trotsky, Zinoviev and Kamenev, and were working to deliberately sabotage Russia's economy. In this way, Stalin was able to create scapegoats for the economic problems that might otherwise have been attributed to inherent problems with the Five-Year Plans.

Secondly, the purges provided a huge reservoir of cheap labour. The majority of the people purged in Stalin's Great Terror were sent to prison camps. Prisoners in Soviet gulags were effectively a source of slave labour. Many of the most important projects commissioned and built during the Five-Year Plans were completed, in large part, by prison workers.

Evidence that Stalin's motives were partly economic can be found in the trial of the Shakhty engineers, the Menshevik Trial of 1931, and the trial of state farm and agricultural officials in 1933. In each case, the accused were tried and found guilty of economic sabotage.

The murder of Kirov

The immediate pretext for the Great Terror was the murder of Kirov. Following the 'Congress of Victors', Stalin had attempted to exclude Kirov from the Politburo by insisting that he stay in Leningrad to supervise the local party. Indeed, Stalin had good reason for wanting to keep Kirov out of Moscow. In 1932, Kirov had helped to defeat him on an important issue concerning Mikhail Riutin, who had circulated a document that was highly critical of Stalin. Stalin was furious and demanded Riutin's execution. In spite of this, both the Central Committee and the Politburo refused to order Riutin's execution. Senior Communists argued that Party members could not be executed for simply opposing Party policy. Stalin viewed this as betrayal.

In December 1934, Kirov was murdered by a lone gunman in his Leningrad headquarters. The Soviet press quickly pinned the murder on Leonid Nikolayev who, they claimed, was working for a secret 'Trotskyite–Zinovievite' terror group who wanted nothing less than the overthrow of the Soviet government. Following the announcement, Zinoviev and Kamenev were arrested for the conspiracy to murder Kirov.

This explanation was convenient for Stalin. The murder had rid him of his most important rival, whilst allowing him to imprison two of his old opponents. What is more, the murder gave Stalin a pretext for hunting down this 'secret terror group'. Finally, Stalin could claim that the murder showed that political dissidents were plotting acts of terror. This justified the execution of Party members who opposed Stalin's policies.

It is impossible to say for certain that Stalin was behind Kirov's murder, but it is certain that Nikolayev was never a member of any secret terrorist organisation. Additionally, there is no evidence of an organised plot to bring down the Soviet government in this period. Rather, some historians have argued that it was Stalin and the NKVD that were behind Kirov's death.

The Great Terror begins: purges under Yagoda and the NKVD

Kirov's death provided Stalin with the excuse he wanted to launch a wave of political terror against the Communist Party. First, within hours of the murder, Stalin had issued a decree authorising the swift execution of political opponents. Secondly, he appointed Yagoda to investigate the murder. Stalin interrogated Nikolayev personally, and following his 'confession' that he was working on the orders of Trotsky, Zinoviev and foreign powers, over one hundred political prisoners, already in NKVD hands, were shot. Thirdly, Stalin sent a secret letter to Communist Party secretaries throughout Russia. The letter, entitled 'Lessons of the events connected with the evil murder of Comrade Kirov', called on all Party organisations to root out Trotskyites wherever they might be found. This purge was focused on Leningrad, and within a few months, between thirty and forty thousand people from this region had been exiled for political crimes.

As Head of the NKVD, Yagoda was responsible for implementing Stalin's new wave of political terror. Yagoda oversaw the arrest, interrogation and trial of Zinoviev and Kamenev. As well as the high-profile show trials, Yagoda also oversaw the arrest of thousands of junior Party members who never featured in high-profile trials. While the scale of the political terror from 1934–1936 was not unusual in Soviet Russia (see table below), this was the first time that the NKVD had turned on the Communist Party itself.

Conclusion

The Communists had always used terror. But the Great Terror was something new. For the first time, political terror was inspired by the paranoia of the leader, and, for the first time, it attacked the ruling party. Terror under Stalin was an integral part of

	Convictions	Executions	Sent to prison camp
1931	180,696	10,651	105,683
1932	141,919	2,728	73,946
1933	239,664	2,154	138,903
1934	78,999	2,056	59,451
1935	267,076	1,229	185,845
1936	274,670	1,118	219,418

Genrikh Yagoda

(1891–1938)

Yagoda became Head of the NKVD in 1934. Prior to this, he had served in the Red Army, and later in the Cheka. He sided with Stalin in the early 1920s due to his belief that Stalin would eventually emerge as the Soviet leader. However, in early 1928, when it looked likely that Bukharin would succeed Lenin, he distanced himself from the General Secretary. Yagoda loved gambling, womanising and luxury. His luxurious lifestyle is evident from the list of possessions made following his arrest in 1937. Amongst his collections he had nine fur coats, three pianos, seventy pairs of silk ladies' panties, and twenty-six pairs of foreign underpants. He was executed following his show trial in 1938.

securing his power over the Party. By finally removing his rivals and those who had personally known Lenin, Stalin's version of socialism – and his version of Party history – would remain unchallenged.

Activity: One big essay

Taking it further

How far do you agree that Stalin had no choice but to launch the Great Terror in order to survive as leader of Soviet Russia?

Your notes for the section on the causes of the Great Terror were in the form of a table. You will need that table for the following activity.

1. Divide into four groups, with each group being allocated one of the following factors that led to the Great Terror:

    ● Congress of Victors

    ● Stalin's paranoia

    ● Terror economics

    ● The murder of Kirov.

2. Each group writes a paragraph (on a large sheet of paper) that explains how their factor caused the Terror. The paragraph should begin with a direct answer to the question – 'What caused Stalin's Great Terror?' This should be followed by three specific examples that support the point. Finally, conclude the paragraph with a sentence that explains why that factor caused the Great Terror. Use different colours for these three sections of the paragraph.

Factor:	Mark out of 10
How clear was the opening point of the paragraph?	
How detailed were the three examples?	
How relevant were the three examples?	
How well did the final sentence explain why this factor caused the Great Terror?	
TOTAL	/40

3. Once each group has written their paragraph, the paragraphs should be read aloud, so that they form one big essay. As each paragraph is being read aloud, the other three groups should assess it, using this table.

4. Once the paragraphs have been read out and assessed, collect together the marks, and award each group a mark out of 120. The group with the highest mark wins.

Chapter 10 **The Great Terror, 1936–1938**

Key questions

- How did the Moscow show trials help to consolidate Stalin's power?
- In what ways did the NKVD change during this period?
- Why did the Great Terror escalate in 1937–1938?

In mid-1936, it appeared that the Great Terror had ended. Stalin commissioned a new constitution which guaranteed freedom of speech, freedom of assembly, equal rights and freedom of the press. Many at the top of the Communist Party breathed a sigh of relief. They believed that it marked the beginning of a new, more tolerant era in Soviet politics. However, nothing could have been further from the truth. Indeed, the years of 1936–1938 are now justly remembered as the height of the Great Terror.

The Moscow show trials

The Great Terror consisted of three parallel strands. The most public aspect of the Great Terror were the three Moscow show trials which finally removed the older high-profile Communists who had once served Lenin. At the same time, the NKVD was reorganised and Yagoda was replaced as People's Commissar for Internal Affairs. The last strand was the mass murder that initially purged the Party and the army, and was then extended to society more generally.

Show trials had been an essential part of justifying Communist government since the end of the Civil War. The purpose of these show trials was not to establish innocence or guilt; the guilt of the non-Communist defendants was assumed from the beginning. Rather, the show trials were a way of publicly proving that the Communists were the only trustworthy party. The three Moscow show trials of 1936–1938 changed this, because, for the first time, well-known Communists themselves were on trial.

The Trial of the Sixteen (1936)

Zinoviev and Kamenev were the main participants of the Trial of the Sixteen. Along with fourteen comrades, they had been in prison for over a year before appearing at the trial. The state charged them with Kirov's murder, as well as plotting to disrupt the Five-Year Plans and conspiring with foreign powers to overthrow the government. Whilst in prison, Zinoviev and Kamenev pleaded their innocence. Zinoviev, in a letter to Stalin, stated 'in no way, in no way, in no way, am I guilty before the Party, before the Central Committee, or before you personally … I beseech you to believe my honest word'. Nonetheless, Zinoviev and Kamenev were 'persuaded' to confess. It is believed that Stalin promised that Zinoviev and Kamenev would be pardoned following a full confession.

> **Take note**
>
> 1. As you work through this section, make brief bullet-pointed notes on each of the Moscow show trials. List the key characters or groups involved, the charges made against them and the result.
>
> 2. As you read about the doctrine of 'sharpening class struggle', make notes on Stalin's ideological justification for the Terror, and the significance of the February–March meeting of the Central Committee.

Timeline

1936	August: Trial of the Sixteen
	September: Yagoda replaced by Nicolai Yezhov as Head of the NKVD
1937	January: Trial of the Seventeen
	February–March: Central Committee Meeting: doctrine of 'sharpening class struggle' accepted; Stalin sets targets for the NKVD
	June: Purge of the Red Army begins
	July: Politburo resolution on anti-Soviet elements (Order No. 00447)
1938	March: Trial of the Twenty-One
	December: Yezhov resigns as Head of the NKVD; replaced by Beria
1939	April: Yezhov arrested

Glossary:

Gulag

A Soviet prison camp. The term emerged from the acronym for the organising body for these camps – the Chief Administration of Corrective Labour Camps and Colonies.

Take note

As you work through this section, make brief bullet-pointed notes on:
1. The reasons for the purges of the Party and the army
2. The extent of these purges
3. The reasons why the Great Terror escalated at this time
4. Those that suffered and those that benefited from the extension of the Great Terror.

Stalin broke his promise, and neither of them was pardoned. The trial judge, Andrei Vyshinsky, summed up: 'Shoot the mad dogs, every last one of them!' Following this sentence, Kamenev and Zinoviev were both shot. Zinoviev begged for mercy until the very last moment, and had to be carried to his execution, weeping. Forty-three other high-ranking Communists and former allies of Zinoviev and Kamenev also disappeared – without trial – around this time.

The Trial of the Seventeen (1937)

The second show trial dealt with Trotsky's former allies. Once again, the charges included plotting with foreign powers, terrorism, sabotage and contact with Trotsky. The Trial of the Seventeen was the first product of Nicolai Yezhov's 'conveyor belt system' of interrogation. Essentially, torture, sleep deprivation and questioning were continued relentlessly until the defendants confessed. Thirteen of the seventeen on trial were executed. The remaining four were sent to **gulags**, where they soon perished.

As in the first show trial, the evidence provided was concocted and forged by the NKVD, but this time the deceit was more obvious. One of the defendants, for example, 'confessed' to murdering Kirov at a time when he was already in prison.

The doctrine of 'sharpening class struggle'

Many within the Communist Party, including senior figures in the Central Committee and the Politburo, were reluctant to try Zinoviev and Kamenev. This reluctance turned into outright opposition when it was rumoured that Stalin's next victim would be Bukharin. Stalin dealt with this opposition by persuading his opponents that Bukharin would not be a defendant at a show trial. Indeed, on 10 September 1937 *Pravda* published an article stating that Vyshinsky had closed his investigation into Bukharin.

Nonetheless, Stalin was still planning Bukharin's trial and execution, and therefore in order to persuade the Party of the necessity of further terror, he proposed a bold new theory. Stalin argued that as socialism advanced, the class struggle intensified. This theory provided the ideological justification for ever-increasing terror. The Communist Party officially adopted this doctrine of 'sharpening class struggle' in the February–March Central Committee meeting of 1937. However, in spite of their loyalty, 70 per cent of those present at the meeting would be executed within three months.

The Trial of the Twenty-One (1938)

The trial of Bukharin, Rykov and their 'accomplices' was the last of the great Moscow show trials. Once again, the defendants were accused of attempting to overthrow socialism and of the murder of Kirov. However, in this final trial Stalin went further, and Bukharin was personally charged with attempting to assassinate Lenin.

Prior to the trial, Bukharin tried to prove his loyalty to Stalin. But Bukharin's efforts were futile. In contrast to previous defendants, he was never tortured. Rather, Stalin threatened to execute his wife and his newborn baby.

The trial was extraordinarily dramatic. Bukharin confessed to 'political responsibility' for the crimes of which he was accused. However, he refused to acknowledge guilt for any of the actual events that had happened. Additionally, Bukharin never confessed to trying to assassinate Lenin. Vyshinsky accused Bukharin and his co-defendants of being 'a foul-smelling heap of human garbage', and he described Bukharin specifically as 'a damnable cross of a fox and a swine'. Bukharin was sentenced to death, but continued to hope for mercy. He wrote to Stalin volunteering to go to America where he 'would smash Trotsky's face in'. But his pleas fell on deaf ears, and soon after his trial, Bukharin was shot. According to contemporary reports, 'Bukharin and Rykov died with curses against Stalin on their lips. They died standing up – not grovelling on the cellar floor, weeping for mercy, like Zinoviev and Kamenev.'

With the execution of Zinoviev, Kamenev and Bukharin, Stalin had shown that there would be no mercy for those who opposed his power. The trials also eliminated the last surviving Communists who could claim to have been close to Lenin and therefore had an authority that was independent of Stalin.

Radicalisation of the NKVD

The years 1936 and 1937 marked a new beginning for the NKVD. Yagoda was replaced as head of the organisation by the more radical Nicolai Yezhov. Indeed, Yagoda was tried alongside Bukharin and Rykov in the final Moscow show trial. The change at the top was reflected in a broader change throughout the NKVD. New, less restrained agents were recruited, in order to speed up and extend the Great Terror.

The fall of Yagoda

Stalin had never fully trusted Yagoda and he also questioned his ability to do his job properly. Stalin thought that Yagoda's handling of the Kirov affair and the Trial of the Sixteen had not been firm enough. Yagoda had also failed to provide evidence against Bukharin and Rykov, and he had incompetently allowed Tomsky to commit suicide before his trial. Stalin's doubts about Yagoda's loyalty stemmed from a secret report of 1928, in which Bukharin had claimed that Yagoda supported the right wing of the Party rather than Stalin. Yezhov, who was Yagoda's second-in-command, played on Stalin's suspicions and suggested that it was time for Yagoda to step down.

It is no surprise, therefore, that following the Trial of the Sixteen, Yagoda was replaced by Yezhov. Two years later, Yagoda himself was sentenced to death following the Trial of the Twenty-One.

A new-style NKVD

Stalin was disappointed by the NKVD's slackness in the early stages of the Great Terror. At the time that Yezhov was appointed People's Commissar for Internal Affairs (Head of the NKVD), Stalin announced that the organisation was 'four years behind'. In order to speed it up, Stalin set targets for arrests,

Take note

As you work through this section, make brief bullet-pointed notes on:
a) How the NKVD changed during this period
b) The effect of these changes on the Great Terror.

Lavrenti Beria

(1899–1953)

Beria joined the Bolsheviks in 1917. Following the Revolution, he worked as a Communist spy in the independent republic of Georgia. After the Soviet invasion of Georgia in 1922, he was appointed Head of the Georgian Cheka. Between 1922 and 1938, he served the regime faithfully as a senior figure in Georgian politics. In 1938, he became Head of the NKVD in Russia. He remained at the top of Soviet politics for the rest of his life. During the Second World War, Stalin tellingly referred to Beria as 'our Himmler', a reference to the leader of the Nazi secret police. Following the war, he was entrusted by Stalin with developing a Russian nuclear weapon. He was executed by the NKVD shortly after Stalin's death.

executions and exiles. Secondly, in 1937, Stalin purged the NKVD itself. Many of the old NKVD had been Communists since the Civil War. Consequently, they felt some loyalty to people such as Bukharin and Rykov. They were also ideologically opposed to the use of indiscriminate terror in a socialist society. New recruits to the NKVD had neither of these scruples. They were either thugs, who enjoyed the violence, or careerist administrators, who met targets in order to gain promotion. Stalin's changes delivered the desired result, and the newly radicalised NKVD set about persecuting 'enemies of the people' with renewed vigour.

Purges and mass murder under Yezhov

The show trials targeted the previous generation of the Communist Party. The purges of 1937 wiped out younger members of the Party, and dealt with 'unreliable elements' within the army. In its final phase, the Great Terror targeted minority groups. Collectively, the period of the purges and mass murder of 1937–1938 were known as '**Yezhovshchina**'

Purges of the Party and the army

In the spring of 1937, Stalin argued that the conspiracy against the Soviet people was not restricted to the forty or so people involved in the show trials. Memos were circulated demanding that Party officials increase their efforts to root out spies and traitors. The NKVD set targets for the numbers of arrests. In the spirit of the Five-Year Plans, these targets were 'over-fulfilled'. Indeed, Yezhov argued that it was 'better to overdo it than not do enough'. The effects on the Party were dramatic. Between 1934 and 1938, some 330,000 Party members were convicted of being enemies of the people.

The Red Army did not escape Stalin's murderous attention. Stalin had never fully trusted the Red Army because the majority of its senior officers had been appointed by his arch rival, Trotsky. For this reason Stalin feared that the military might try to seize power. In June 1937 eight Generals were tried. Following their brutal torture at the hands of the NKVD, the Generals confessed to treason. In the following eighteen months, 34,000 soldiers were purged from the army. Historian Donald Rayfield comments that 'the death toll was comparable to that of a major war'.

Mass murder

The show trials had provided 'evidence' that there was an anti-Soviet conspiracy, involving large numbers of people across Russia. In response, the Politburo issued NKVD Order No. 00447, demanding the removal of 'anti-Soviet elements' from Russian society. The NKVD produced a list of over 250,000 people who were believed to be involved in anti-Soviet activity.

It is commonly assumed that the NKVD kept large numbers of people under surveillance and chose its victims. However, in reality, the Russian people themselves collaborated enthusiastically with the state-sponsored persecution. Many Russians chose to denounce their friends and neighbours to the secret police. In some ways, this was a survival strategy and an attempt to prove their loyalty by reporting their friends. However, there were also other motives. Indeed, it was not uncommon for workers to denounce their bosses, hoping that once their boss was removed they would be promoted. The same logic was at work in terms of housing. Nonetheless, the NKVD played a significant role in increasing the scope of the Terror. Regional officials badgered the central offices with requests for higher targets in order to be allowed to arrest more people.

Conclusion

At the end of 1938, the Great Terror subsided, but the NKVD would claim two more high-profile victims. The first was Yezhov. He resigned as Head of the NKVD in November 1938 and was arrested in April of the following year. His alleged crimes included terrorism, spying for foreign countries and moral degeneracy. He argued that his only crime was killing too few Russians. In February 1940, he was executed. His replacement, Lavrenti Beria, compiled a list of 346 of Yezhov's 'associates' who were also to be shot. The final victim was Trotsky. The NKVD had been pursuing Trotsky since 1930. Where Yagoda and Yezhov had failed, Beria succeeded. On 20 August 1940, Ramón Mercader, an NKVD agent, broke into Trotsky's house in Mexico and killed him with an ice-pick. Beria and Stalin were well suited. Indeed, Beria famously remarked 'when you stop murdering people by the millions, they start to get ideas'.

Taking it further

The Great Terror is usually considered to have started following Kirov's death in 1934. Nonetheless, terror was an essential part of Communist rule during the collectivisation drives of 1928 onwards. For this reason, some historians have argued that the Great Terror actually started in 1928.

Write two paragraphs, one arguing that the Great Terror started in 1934, the other arguing that it began in 1928. Ensure that your arguments are backed up with specific detail and clearly explain the points they make.

Activity: Timelines of Terror

This chapter has discussed three related aspects of the Great Terror. In order to better understand the links between these three strands:

1. Copy the following timelines (your timelines should be at least A3 size):

	1936	1937	1938	1939
Moscow show trials				
NKVD				
Purges and mass murder				

2. Using your notes on this chapter, add key events to your timelines. For example, mark on the changes in leadership of the NKVD.

3. Add detail to your timelines. For example, explain why the leadership of the NKVD changed.

4. Using a different-coloured pen, draw lines to show causal links between the events on different timelines. For example, the changes in the NKVD could be seen as a cause of the escalation of the purges.

5. Ensure that as well as marking each link on the timeline, you also write a brief explanation of how one event caused the other.

Chapter 11 **Consequences of the Terror**

Key questions

- How did the Great Terror change Russian society?
- How did the Great Terror affect Stalin's economic plans?
- How did Stalin use the Great Terror to consolidate his power?

The NKVD always made arrests at the dead of night. Their official procedure was to storm a suspect's apartment between the hours of two and three in the morning. This guaranteed that their activities would not be missed and would strike fear into the hearts of all within earshot. By 1937, the Great Terror was so widespread that many Communists kept bags packed in anticipation of their imminent arrest. In these circumstances, it was impossible to live a normal life. Friends betrayed one another, children disowned their parents, and people changed their identities to avoid capture. No aspect of Russian life was unchanged as the Terror engulfed the society, the economy and the politics of the nation.

Take note

As you work through this chapter, draw a spider diagram to show the social, economic and political consequences of the Great Terror. For each general point you include on the diagram, add a supporting specific example.

The social impact of the Great Terror

The Great Terror was so far-reaching that it changed the daily routines of life – it shattered families, ruined careers and forced others to disown their pasts.

Who were the victims?

The focus of the Great Terror changed as time went on. In 1935, the focus was on members of the Leningrad Party and bourgeois specialists. In 1936 and early 1937, the purge was extended to former oppositionists and the current leadership of the Communist Party, NKVD and army. In the case of the army, 35,000 officers were either exiled or shot, and over 23,000 NKVD agents were killed. Between 1935 and the end of 1936, Yagoda's NKVD convicted over half a million people. Of this, approximately 2,300 were shot, and 405,000 were sent to prison camps. Others died in police custody or disappeared without an official explanation.

Between 1937 and 1938 – a period the western historian Donald Rayfield has described as the 'Yezhov bloodbath' – the violence became more widespread. It has been estimated that 10 per cent of adult males were executed or sent to the labour camps. Nonetheless, the persecution was directed against specific social groups. First, it affected the urban and educated population far more than manual workers or peasants. Indeed, those most at risk were between the ages of 30 and 45, in managerial or professional positions. In terms of gender, only 5 per cent of all of those arrested were women. The women most likely to be affected by the Terror were single, or were relatives of men that had been purged. The Great Terror also discriminated on the basis of nationality. Indeed, the NKVD had specific targets for the numbers of Poles, Romanians and Latvians to be persecuted. Overall, at the height of the Terror, around 1.5 million were arrested by the NKVD. Of these, over 635,000 were exiled and over 680,000 people were shot.

Terrorised families

In the central districts of Moscow, some apartment blocks became entirely deserted during 1937. Arrests had devastating effects on entire families, with wives of top Party officials being likely to be arrested along with their husbands. In the majority of cases, however, the wives of 'enemies of the people' merely lost their jobs. Once a husband had been arrested, it was common for his wife to petition the authorities demanding their loved one's release. In some cases, the queues of people outside government buildings demanding to know what had happened to their husbands rivalled the queues at shoe shops. However, in most cases, wives were not considered to be enemies of the people merely because they believed that their husbands were innocent.

The older children of those arrested were likely to be expelled from university. School-age children were subjected to ritual humiliation by teachers and peers in the classroom. Furthermore, it was expected that the children of those arrested would publicly disown and renounce their parents. Indeed, during 1937–1938, formal renunciations formed part of both everyday school life and the programme of Komsomol.

Eliminating the old elite

The Great Terror had a marked effect on local Party organisations, and on factory management. In each case, the existing elite was 'washed away' and replaced by a new, more loyal group of leaders.

In Russia's regions, the example of the Moscow show trials was replicated on a smaller scale. At the Yaroslavl trial, workers from the local rubber factory accused the management of malpractice. The local trials were heavily publicised, and in some cases the entire workforce of the factory involved would be present during the trial to watch their former bosses being publicly humiliated. The Stakhanovite movement were highly active during the purges. They held monthly meetings where criticisms of the management could be aired openly. As a result, the existing management of Soviet industry were scapegoated for problems, sacked for being 'wreckers', and in many cases, turned over to the NKVD.

1937 witnessed a massive purge of the existing Communist Party membership. Following the February–March Central Committee meeting that had authorised the extension of the Terror, the spring elections were used to purge Communists in positions of authority. For the first time in fifteen years, Stalin issued no lists instructing Party members who to elect to senior positions. Consequently, the Party administration was temporarily paralysed as Party members, desperate to avoid falling into the hands of the NKVD, scrutinised candidates for high office. In effect, junior members of the Party took on the role of the NKVD, interrogating those who sought election and unmasking many as 'enemies of the people'. In some areas, elections lasted for weeks. In the Yaroslavl factory, for example, the Party Committee's 800 members attended meetings every evening for over a month in order to decide who to elect.

A similar process was employed to elect the leaders of Russia's trade unions.

Candidates were required to disclose detailed biographical information. They were then cross-examined concerning their real class identity and their service to the Party. Many were then labelled 'enemies of the people'.

Forging new identities

One way of escaping the Terror was to create an entirely new identity. Kulaks, priests, former Nepmen and people who had once been part of Russia's nobility were the likely targets of the NKVD. Consequently, many in these groups reinvented themselves as factory workers, or administrators in Stalin's new industries. Simply working in a factory was not enough. For the 'former people' it was essential to invent an entire family history. This could be done in a variety of ways. First, women could change their class origins by marrying genuine members of the working class. For example, Anna Dubova, the daughter of a kulak, moved to Moscow, married a working man and enrolled in a factory school in order to escape being exiled. Secondly, forged identity papers were readily available throughout Russia. Official documents contained no photographs and therefore could be easily faked. A third strategy was to destroy existing identity documents and, upon arrival in a new area, bribe a local official to invent a new working class biography. The most high-profile example of one of these 'hidden enemies' was Vladimir Gromov. Gromov was sentenced to ten years in a gulag for impersonating a prize-winning architect and engineer. He had used his false identity to persuade the government to pay him a million roubles in advance for designing an important government project.

The economic impact of the Great Terror

Officially, the Great Terror was designed to boost economic production by eradicating 'wreckers' and saboteurs. In practice, however, the Great Terror wreaked economic havoc. During the Terror, Communist Party members felt compelled to lie about economic facts in order to give the impression that the government had met its targets and to avoid arrest and execution. Consequently, it was impossible to plan effectively because the truth was consistently distorted. Secondly, purges within Gosplan eliminated many of Russia's most experienced economic planners, and at a local level the Terror wiped away many competent industrial managers.

The effect of the purges in the Donbas region of Ukraine typifies the economic impact of the Great Terror more generally. In 1929, the Donbas region accounted for over 77 per cent of Russia's coal production. From the summer of 1936 to the autumn of 1938, more than a quarter of the management in the coalmines were purged. As a result, the rate of coal production fell dramatically. Coal production, which had virtually doubled between 1928 and 1932, and doubled again between 1932 and 1936, barely grew from the beginning of the Great Terror to 1940.

The slowdown in economic growth experienced in the Donbas region was experienced throughout Russia. Indeed, the western historian Alec Nove argues that the relative failure of the Third Five-Year Plan was a direct result

Taking it further

Historians have taken a variety of approaches to analysing the Great Terror. Some have attempted to assess its impact through statistics. Others have focused on personal accounts of life during the Terror. What are the advantages and disadvantages of statistical data as a historical source for understanding the Terror? What are the advantages and disadvantages of personal recollections?

Coal production in the Donbas region (millions of tonnes)

Year	Production
1928	27
1932	45
1936	80
1940	82

of the Great Terror which 'swept away managers, technicians, statisticians and planners, leading to a shortage of trained workers'.

The political impact of the Great Terror

The Great Terror served a political purpose. It publicly established the guilt and corruption of those who had once opposed Stalin. Additionally, at a local level, it provided scapegoats for popular discontent, as well as drama in the otherwise mundane lives of Soviet citizens.

Removing rivals

The three Moscow show trials 'proved', once and for all, that everyone who had opposed Stalin had done so for corrupt reasons. Zinoviev, Kamenev, Bukharin and former Trotskyists were all exposed as traitors who had worked for foreign governments and assassins who had plotted the death of the popular hero, Kirov. Following these trials, Stalin moved to eliminate the followers of those who had been convicted.

Populist Terror

Stalin's economic plans had obvious failings and the 1930s was a time of shortages, hard work and strict discipline. In order to divert people's attention from these problems, Stalin encouraged Russia's 'little people' to hold their bosses to account. The resulting local show trials targeted government employees, Party officials and factory managers. The defendants were charged with a variety of crimes which indicate the strength of discontent during the period. For example, in Kazan, Communist officials were publicly tried for misusing government funds. The trials attacked the luxurious lifestyles enjoyed by the Kazan Party bosses. Notably, no crime had actually been committed because luxury was part-and-parcel of the lifestyle of the Communist elite. Nonetheless, the Party bosses were purged and local people felt that their accusations had been justified.

Conclusion

Stalin emerged from the Great Terror stronger than ever before. The Terror had removed any potential threats within the military, economic and political leadership of Russia. Additionally, the Terror provided scapegoats that explained the failure of Stalin's economic plans, the cruelty of domestic policy and the gap between the vision of socialist Russia and the everyday reality of queues and shortages. Nonetheless, Stalin's security came at an unimaginable price. Estimates of the numbers executed vary from 500,000 to 1,500,000. In addition to this, some 2,000,000 of those exiled to the camps died between 1937 and 1938. While there may never be a definitive count of the human cost of Stalin's rule, there can be no doubt that Stalin was one of the greatest mass murderers in European history.

Activity: Axes of Terror

This activity asks you to consider which of the consequences of the Great Terror was the most significant. Significance can be measured by considering the number of people affected by an event or process, and the severity of that effect.

1. Take three small cards and label them: 'Social consequences of the Great Terror', 'Economic consequences of the Great Terror' and 'Political consequences of the Great Terror'.

2. Draw these two axes on a large piece of paper:

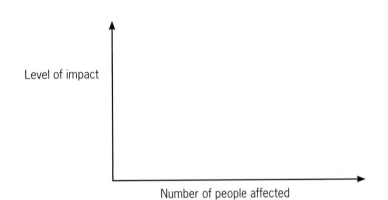

3. First, consider how many people were affected by each of the social, economic and political consequences of the Great Terror. Place your three cards in appropriate places along the bottom axis of the graph. For example, if you feel that economic disruption affected very few people, you might place your 'Economic consequences' card in the left-hand corner of the graph.

4. Next, consider the level of impact caused by each of these consequences. Move your three cards up the graph to indicate the relative impact. For example, if you feel that, although economic disruption affected very few people, for those people the effects were severe, you might place your 'Economic consequences' card at the top left-hand corner of the graph.

5. Next to each card, write three bullet-points explaining that position of the card on the graph.

6. Finally, make a judgement about whether the social, economic, or political consequences of the Great Terror were most significant. Write a paragraph explaining your decision. Remember to use specific examples to support your argument.

Chapter 12 Terror in Stalin's final years, 1941–1953

Key questions
- What methods did Stalin use to remove perceived opponents to his rule?
- Why did Stalin continue to use political terror in his final years?
- How did Stalin's Terror change over time?

Stalin had a number of official nicknames. During the 1940s, he became known as 'leader, teacher, friend', 'true friend and dependable brother-in-arms' and 'wise and dearly beloved'. His most bizarre nickname was perhaps 'best friend of the cowherds and milkmaids'. Rather than simply being the leader or the General Secretary, Stalin was put forward as a beloved companion. However, the 'friend of the cowherd' still had enemies – the 'enemies of the people'. During his last years, Stalin perceived his enemies to be many and various. He believed that they included many of Russia's Jews, senior officials of the Leningrad Party, heroes of the Second World War and, finally, the doctors at the Kremlin.

The NKVD at war

For Stalin, the Second World War was a battle with enemies within, just as much as it was a battle with Germany. Beria's NKVD was used to police Russian society in order to ensure that those 'hampering' the war effort were eliminated.

Purging the Red Army

At the beginning of the war, Russia suffered heavy defeats. Consequently, Stalin ordered a purge of the top ranks of the Red Army. First, from February 1937 to November 1938, Stalin authorised the execution of almost 39,000 army officers and 3,000 naval officers. Secondly, in 1941 Stalin purged 'military intelligence'. He blamed them for not alerting him to Germany's plans to invade Russia. Thirdly, generals who had performed badly against the German army were shot. However, as the war went on, Stalin was forced to stop this policy because Russia needed all the military expertise available in order to fight Hitler. Indeed, two generals who had been tortured in a gulag were released and sent out to lead troops against the German army.

The enemy within

The NKVD drew up a list of people within Russia who might be sympathetic to the Germans and therefore needed to be dealt with. First, all political prisoners in regions under threat from German invasion were executed. Secondly, entire people groups were exiled. For example, the Kalmyks, an ethnic group of over 130,000 people, were forcibly moved to Siberia for fear that they would welcome a German invasion. By 1953, only 53,000 survived because of the brutal treatment they received in Siberia. A second example

Take note

As you work through this chapter, complete the following table:

	What happened?	Why did Stalin attack this group?
Purging the Red Army		
The enemy within		
Prisoners of war		
Purge of the Jews		
The Leningrad Affair		
The Doctors' Plot		

Timeline

1941	USSR enters the Second World War Senior generals punished for Russian losses
1944	Kalmyks and Chechens exiled
1945	Prisoners of war return to the USSR, and are interrogated and exiled
1946–9	Purges of the Jews
1949	The Leningrad Affair
1952	The Doctors' Plot
1953	March: Stalin's death; Beria's execution

were the Chechen people. Beria ordered that all 460,000 Chechens were to be moved in seven days. But harsh weather meant that this was just not possible. Therefore all those Chechen people who had not been moved were locked in stables and barns – and burned alive.

Prisoners of war

At the end of the Second World War, the Yalta Conference agreed that prisoners of war would be returned to their country of origin. As many as 1.5 million Soviet soldiers who had been held captive by the Germans, returned to their homeland, many against their will. Rather than being welcomed as heroes, the returning soldiers were immediately interrogated and exiled. In Stalin's eyes these soldiers were traitors. They were guilty of disobeying Stalin's direct order not to allow themselves to be captured, and this 'breach of discipline' was punished with years of hard labour in concentration camps in Siberia. The returning prisoners of war joined other prison inmates who had heroically escaped from German concentration camps during the war only to be exiled on their return, accused of spying.

Stalin's final purges

Following the war, Stalin continued to use terror as a method of totalitarian political control. He became increasingly paranoid about potential rivals and deluded himself into believing that he was shortly to be the victim of sinister conspiracies.

Purge of the Jews

Having won the war, Stalin was highly suspicious of his former allies. Indeed, he was concerned about all of his citizens who had contacts with the outside world. Any 'cosmopolitan' Russian was a potential spy and traitor. Stalin believed that the Jews were fundamentally cosmopolitan and had more loyalty to fellow Jews than they did to Russia. Consequently, he launched a purge against 'cosmopolitan elements' in Russian society – a purge that essentially victimised the Jews. For example, in 1945, 12 per cent of senior managers in the government and industry were Jewish. This had fallen to 4 per cent in 1951. All of the Jews in sensitive areas, such as diplomacy and Russia's military, were removed.

The Leningrad Affair

Stalin had long been concerned that he had never stamped his authority on Russia's second city. In 1949, he commented that Leningrad acted like it was 'an island in the Pacific'. Subsequently, over a thousand Leningrad Party members were sacked. Two hundred of these were arrested and charged with being traitors to the Motherland. As in the Great Terror, confessions were extracted using the NKVD's 'conveyor belt system'.

The Doctors' Plot

In the final years of his life, Stalin became increasingly concerned that those closest to him, including NKVD chief Beria, were trying to kill him. Stalin's personal physician, Professor Vladimir Vinogradov, aroused his suspicion by suggesting that the only cure for Stalin's ill-health was to reduce his workload. Following this diagnosis, Professor Vinogradov and over thirty other top physicians were arrested. The NKVD charged the doctors with the assassination of leading members of the Communist Party, and of plotting to poison Stalin. Fortunately for the physicians concerned, Stalin died before the purge could escalate. Soon after his death, the doctors were released.

Conclusion

Stalin's motives for the use of political terror following 1941 were various. First, as in the Great Terror of the late 1930s, Stalin was looking for scapegoats. He blamed early defeats in the Second World War on his military generals. Secondly, his motives were economic. Prisoners of war were ideal slave labour because they were generally young, fit and physically strong. Additionally, Stalin's paranoia cannot be overlooked. Prisoners of war and Jews had, in Stalin's mind, too many connections with the outside world and too much knowledge of life outside the USSR. Consequently, Stalin refused to trust them. Old age also took its toll on Stalin's outlook. He knew that he was in his final years. He was also aware that he was not as energetic or quick-witted as he had once been. Therefore, he suspected that his rivals would take advantage of his decline and remove him from power.

Activity: Spot the wrecker!

During the Great Terror, Russian citizens were at risk of arrest for a variety of reasons. People's personal histories were scrutinised by agents of the NKVD for telltale signs that they were Trotskyists, saboteurs or wreckers.

1. In pairs, you will play the part of NKVD agents working in 1937. You have been given biographies of six possible suspects. It is your job to go through the information on these suspects and identify evidence that they are enemies of the people. Annotate each card to show areas of concern. As an example, the first biography has been annotated for you.

Name: Filip

Year of birth: 1894

Occupation: Chairman of the Tambov region Communist Party

Social class: Working class

Personal history: Joined the Communist Party in 1921. Prior to this, was a member of the Mensheviks. Attended the 1934 Communist Party Congress and was elected Chairman of the Tambov Region Communist Party. Complained about collectivisation in 1929.

No problem here!

Suspicious: why didn't he join at the time of the Revolution?

Suspicious: attended the Congress of Victors where there was a rebellion against Stalin.

Suspicious: opposed Communist Party policy.

Suspicious: the Mensheviks were a counter-revolutionary political party and were banned by Lenin in 1921.

> **Source 12.1: A description of the torture of Viktor Abakumov, a senior member of the Leningrad Communist Party and member of the NKVD**
>
> Abakumov's torments were to last three and a half years. Three interrogators worked with rawhide whips to generate enough material to keep Stalin happy. Abakumov, as Stalin reminded his henchmen, needed extra beating to break him. Abakumov was first made to confess to beating his own prisoners. Abakumov was put into leg-irons and handcuffed, he had no cell mates, he was hungry and cold. On April 18th 1952, Abakumov appealed to Beria 'I have never ever seen such bestiality'.
>
> Taken from: *Stalin and his Hangmen* by Donald Rayfield (2004)

Taking it further

In order to gain a better understanding of the treatment of gulag prisoners during this period, read *One Day in the Life of Ivan Denisovich* by Alexander Solzhenitsyn (1962). The story is set in a Soviet labour camp in the 1950s and describes a single day in the life of a prisoner.

Name: Yevgenyi

DOB: 1912

Occupation: Factory worker

Social class: Working class

Personal history: Born in Moscow to a large Jewish family. Joined the Communist Party in 1930. Moved to Donbas region in 1935 as a voluntary worker. In 1935, was awarded a medal for exceeding production targets in the Donbas coalmines. In 1936, represented the mine at the All-Russia Congress of Stakhanovites. In early 1937, reported three managers at the mine for wrecking activities. Divorced wife after discovering she was related to a kulak.

Name: Natalia

DOB: 1918

Occupation: Unemployed

Social class: unsure - see below

Personal history: Born in Ukraine. Arrived in Leningrad in 1935 with no identity papers. Applied to the local Soviet for new identity documents, claiming to be the daughter of a factory worker. Married a factory manager in 1936. Joined the factory as a cake-decorator. Husband arrested for wrecking activities in early 1937. Sacked from the factory following husband's arrest. Repeatedly petitioned the NKVD for husband's release.

Name: Valentin

DOB: 1908

Occupation: Red Army officer

Social class: Working class

Personal history: Born to kulak parents in Tsaritsyn. Joined OGPU in 1923. During 1925 arrested twenty priests. Promoted to Section Leader of the NKVD in 1927. In 1929 joined the Twenty-five-thousanders and mercilessly organised the exile of kulak farmers. During the 1932–1934 famine he executed a family of peasants for stealing grain. Worked as Yagoda's assistant from 1932 to 1936. Left the NKVD in 1936 to join the Red Army on hearing of the possible threat of German invasion.

Name: Vladimir

DOB: 1892

Occupation: Factory manager

Social class: Bourgeois

Personal history: Born to bourgeois parents in Moscow. Father owned a textile factory. Began managing textile factory in 1913. Worked for the Communists as a 'bourgeois specialist' during the Civil War. Managed a small factory during the NEP. An enthusiastic supporter of the Five-Year Plans. Joined the Communist Party in 1921. Moved to Leningrad in 1935 and quickly became a leading member of the Leningrad Party.

Name: Nikolai

DOB: 1879

Occupation: Gosplan Administrator

Social class: Intellectual

Personal history: Joined the Communist Party in 1917. Served under Trotsky in the Civil War. In 1924, joined the Left Opposition. In 1926, joined the United Opposition. In 1927, opposed the expulsion of Trotsky from the Communist Party. He was expelled from the Party in 1927, but readmitted in 1928, due to his support for Stalin's economic plans. During the First Five-Year Plan, worked in heavy industry department of Gosplan.

2. Place the cards in a line to show which suspects you believe to be the most dangerous, and which you believe to be most loyal to Stalin. Arrange the cards in order of suspicion, the most suspicious on the far left, the least on the far right.

3. Now imagine it is 1949. Examine the suspects again. Repeat the previous activity using your knowledge of the Terror in Stalin's final years. How does the order change? Why does the order change?

Activity: Continuity and change

As the previous activity has suggested, the Great Terror progressed over time.

1. Complete the following table to show how the Great Terror differed under Yagoda, Yezhov and Beria.

	Dates in power	Relationship with Stalin	Extent of the Terror	Methods used by the NKVD	Who was persecuted?
Yezhov					
Yagoda					
Beria					

2. Having completed the table, answer the following questions:

- How did the Terror change over time?
- In what ways did the Terror remain constant?

Chapter 13 The art of power – Socialist Realism and the cult of personality

Key questions
- How can Socialist Realism be defined?
- What were the key features of the 'cults of personality'?
- How did Stalin use art as a form of social control?

Stalin's ambition was limitless. A revolutionary transformation of the economy was only the starting point. Stalin dreamed of creating a whole new breed of human being, to be known as *Homo Sovieticus* – Soviet Man. To this end, he enlisted the arts and Soviet artists, for, in his eyes, artists were nothing less than 'engineers of the human soul'.

Russian art and culture before Stalin

In the early days of Communist rule, the Soviet authorities were prepared to tolerate a great deal of diversity in revolutionary art and culture. Art during the 1920s was revolutionary in a number of senses. First, it was revolutionary in that it was deliberately experimental and different from traditional art forms. Leading artist Kasimir Malevich produced abstract paintings such as 'Black Square' – literally a black square. In music, Léon Theremin invented the world's first electronic musical instrument – the theremin. Lenin was so impressed by the new instrument that he attempted to learn to play it. Finally, Soviet cinema was decidedly experimental. Dziga Vertov, who was in charge of the Russian newsreel, *Kino Pravda*, used techniques such as slow-motion, freeze-frames and running films backwards – in films that had no characters, no sets, no actors and no plot.

Secondly, Russian art was revolutionary in the sense that it celebrated modern industrial technology. Pictures were made up of abstract geometric shapes that recalled factory buildings. In music, Alexander Mosolov wrote pieces such as 'The Iron Foundry' and a ballet entitled 'Steel'. Finally, Russian art in the 1920s was revolutionary because it promoted the revolutionary government. Sergei Eisenstein, for example, made a trilogy of films celebrating the struggle of the workers against the Tsar.

Timeline

1929	All-Union Co-operative of Workers in Representational Arts founded
1932	Decree on the Reformation of Literary–Artistic Organisations
1934	First All-Union Congress of Soviet Writers – official adoption of Socialist Realism
1935	General Plan for the Reconstruction of Moscow
1936	Committee for Art Affairs (KPDI) established
1938	Publication of *The Short Course of the History of the All-Union Communist Party* and *The Short Biography of Stalin*

Take note

As you work through the first three sections of this chapter (up to the heading 'Art for the leaders'), try the following method of recording information:
1. Divide your paper into two columns, with the left-hand column only a third of the width of the right-hand column.
2. In the left-hand column, write only the section headings and the points that you think are most important. Try and write as few words as possible in this column.
3. In the right-hand column, make detailed notes, with specific examples.
4. Once you have finished each of the three sections, rule a line across the entire page and continue the next section underneath.

Reconstructing the arts

In 1930, Stalin expressed his discontent with Soviet art. In an article in *The Bolshevik,* he argued that revolutionary art, properly understood, should express government opinion rather than individual creativity. Moreover, according to Stalin, much Soviet art meant nothing to the average peasant or worker. Abstract shapes, films with no plot, and music with no melody, were simply incomprehensible to the Soviet masses.

Reorganising Soviet literature

Soviet literature was officially reorganised in April 1932, following the 'Decree on the Reformation of Literary-Artistic Organisations'. The Decree established the Union of Soviet Writers, which attempted to define the style appropriate for Russian authors. In 1932, Ivan Kulik, President of the Ukrainian Writers' Union, argued that all Soviet writers who were genuinely behind the revolution should adopt a style that he described as 'Socialist Realism'.

When the first All-Union Congress of Soviet Writers met in 1934, they officially adopted Socialist Realism as the new Soviet style. They praised works such as Fyodor Gladkov's *Cement* – a novel telling the story of a cement factory worker – as the epitome of the new style.

Socialist Realism

At the first All-Union Congress of Soviet Writers, the phrase 'Socialist Realism' was used 228 times. Nonetheless, it proved tricky to define. Kulik described it as mixing art that aims to provide 'a true reflection of reality' with art that 'tries to participate in the building of socialism'. Others described it as art with 'both feet on the solid ground of life'. The Congress believed that Socialist Realist art had to be full of *Partynost* (Party spirit), *Narodnost* (national spirit) and *Ideinost* (art that reflected the new thinking).

In practice, it was difficult to see what Socialist Realism would actually mean. Nevertheless, following the Congress, Soviet artists set about enthusiastically 'educating the workers in the spirit of communism'. The emphasis on 'art for the workers' led to a shift from art that was experimental to a more traditional approach. Abstract art came under heavy criticism, and the new paintings were 'realistic' in the sense that they looked like photographs. As the style developed, it became clear that Socialist Realism was an attempt to use art forms to sell government economic and social policy to the Russian people.

Art for the workers

In 1929, the All-Union Co-operative of Workers in Representational Arts was established. In many ways, the new organisation worked in the same way as the Five-Year Plans. Additionally, it refocused the attention of artists on the successes of government economic policy.

Artists as workers

In the spirit of the Five-Year Plan, members of the All-Union Co-operative were set targets regarding the number of works of art they were expected to produce and the subject matter they were expected to tackle. In July 1930, two hundred artists were sent to work on collective farms and Five-Year Plan construction sites. During their two-month placements, they were expected to record the heroic work that they witnessed. In 1936, the Party tightened its grip on artists, setting up the Committee for Art Affairs, or KPDI. The KPDI, under the leadership of Yezhov, immediately began a purge of Soviet artists. According to Alexander Gerasimov – Stalin's favourite painter – there was a new 'creative atmosphere of enthusiasm among the entire mass of artists'. Needless to say, the artists who were sent to the gulag saw things differently.

Inspirational art

Socialist Realist art was designed to inspire the workers. Artists were required to 'reflect in art the spirit and experiences of life out on the major sites of socialist industry'. Artists created sculptures celebrating the new Moscow ball-bearing factory and the Dnieper power station. In the first case, Soviet sculptors produced a ball-bearing ten metres in diameter. The second sculpture created a model of the Dnieper dam that was more than seventy metres wide.

The Five-Year Plans were also the focus of many posters and paintings. For example, Gustavs Klucis was commissioned to produce the poster called 'In the Storm of the Third Year of the Five-Year Plan' which portrayed heroic workers mining and Valentine Kataev wrote a stirring celebration of the production of steel in his novel, *Forward, Oh Time!*

Joy in the village!

Russian artists also attempted to glorify the achievements of collectivisation. The painter Samuil Adlivankin, for example, depicted a crowd of joyful peasants in his painting 'Voting to Expel the Kulak from the Collective Farm'. Equally, Dziga Vertov's film, *Three Songs about Lenin*, described the way in which new technology had created farms in the desert. A final example is the famous painting 'They are Writing About Us in *Pravda*' by Aleksei Vasilev, which depicts happy peasants eating a plentiful meal while a party worker with a motorbike reads to them from *Pravda*. Socialist Realism continually stressed the plenty enjoyed in the villages and the easy availability of new technology on Soviet farms in spite of the fact that collectivisation had actually caused untold hardship and famine.

Cities fit for heroes

Urban workers were the totalitarian regime's new heroes. For this reason, Stalin commissioned the Union of Soviet Architects to redesign Russia's cities. The new cities were designed to 'demonstrate that there is no country in the world as blessed as the Soviet Union'. Moscow was the first city to enjoy a Socialist Realist makeover. Following the 1935 General Plan for the Reconstruction of Moscow, Stalin's architects attempted to create 'a truly socialist city'. The Plan followed the example of the Five-Year Plans by trying to transform the city in a very short period. One of the successes of the Plan was the Moscow metro stations. These were not simply underground railway stations, they were designed like palaces, decorated with grand columns made from marble and illuminated by crystal chandeliers. Government

Source 13.1: An extract from *Cement* by Fyodor Gladkov (1924)

Nearby, behind the tower to the right, a regiment of Red soldiers was standing at ease. Once he had stood so with them. How long ago was that? And now he was here, once more a factory worker and, besides, the leader of the Party Group. The works! What strength had been put into it, and what struggle! But here it was – a giant, a beauty!

Source 13.2 An extract from *Forward, Oh Time* by Valentine Kataev (1934)

To make life happy, it was not enough to say good words. It was not enough. One needed steel, steel, steel! With steel, there will be a new, happy life, a life that has never been before, a life that has never been seen before!

buildings such as the People's Commissariat for Defence and the Frunze Military Academy were also built in a grand style.

Art for the leaders

As well as focusing on heroic workers and peasants, Soviet leaders also featured heavily in Socialist Realist art. Paintings, novels, photographs and even histories were produced glorifying Stalin and rewriting history to prove his great genius.

The 'Myth of Two Leaders'

By the late 1930s, Soviet history was being extensively rewritten. Stalin then created the 'Myth of Two Leaders' – putting himself alongside Lenin. The myth greatly emphasised Stalin's role in the early days of Communist rule, and eliminated other important Communists, particularly Trotsky, from Party history. It implied that during Lenin's lifetime, Stalin had been his right-hand man, and aimed to show that Stalin was 'the Lenin of today'.

Remaking the past

Two histories, both published in 1938, were central to creating the new myth. Both were edited by Stalin himself. *The Short Course of the History of the All-Union Communist Party* and *The Short Biography of Stalin* erased Trotsky from Party history and made the most of Stalin's contributions to the Communist Party.

Where the histories led, artists and novelists followed. Maria Krickova's *The Tale of Lenin* tells the story of Lenin's death. Lenin is described as the sun, Stalin as the light that overcomes the darkness – which represents Trotsky. Socialist Realist paintings created fictional historical situations from the years 1917–1924 in which Stalin was always at Lenin's side. Finally, photographs were altered, erasing Trotsky, Zinoviev and other former leaders from the early days of Communist government.

It was not only the early days that were changed. Communists who had been purged during the 1930s were also removed from Soviet art and history. For example, Dmitri Nalbandyan's painting of 'Stalin, Kirov and Yagoda at the White Sea Canal' had to be repainted, following Yagoda's arrest, in order to remove him from the scene.

The cult of personality

During the 1930s and 1940s, there were in effect two cults of personality, one of Lenin, the other of Stalin. Officially, Lenin remained the more important figure, with Stalin describing himself as the pupil and Lenin as the teacher. The Lenin cult of the 1930s continued to use the religious language that had surrounded Lenin since his death. For example, in Dziga Vertov's film *Three Songs about Lenin*, Lenin is described as 'a ray of truth' and as a father who brought life to the deserts. In 1930, Lenin's tomb in Moscow was extensively rebuilt. Indeed, the streets around the tomb were widened, with many historic buildings being torn down in order to allow massive parades to pass the mausoleum. The Lenin cult was crucial to the totalitarian regime. It created a powerful new symbol and new rituals which replaced Christianity

Take note

As you work through this section, make two lists – one listing all of the ways in which art was used to glorify Stalin, and the other listing all of the ways in which events from history were used to emphasise Stalin's importance.

Source 13.3: An extract from *Joseph Stalin: A Short Biography* by G. F. Alexandov et al. (1951)

'I recall the year 1917' says Stalin, 'when, after my wandering from one prison and place of exile to another, I was transferred by the will of the Party to Leningrad. There in the society of Russian workers, and in direct contact with Comrade Lenin, the great teacher of the proletarian of all countries … I first learnt what it meant to be one of the leaders of the great Party of the working class.' Stalin was at the centre of all the practical activities of the Party. Together with Lenin, he took part in the All-Russian Conference of the Party Organisation. Together with Lenin, he organised the historic demonstration of June 18. After July 1917, when Lenin was forced to go into hiding, Stalin directly guided the work of the Central Committee.

and allowed Russian citizens to form an emotional bond with the regime.

From the mid-1930s Soviet artists and journalists generated a 'cult of Stalin', which linked to Lenin. Indeed, paintings used a variety of devices to imply that the ghost of Lenin was, in some sense, always with Stalin. For example, in 'Long Live the Stalinist Order of Heroes and Stakhanovites' by Gustavs Klucis, the living Stalin stands immediately in front of a bust of the dead Lenin. *Pravda* and other Communist newspapers praised Stalin's wisdom on a daily basis. It was even suggested that the works of Stalin and Lenin should be read together, and a new ideology was born: 'Marxism–Leninism–Stalinism'. Additionally, Stalin's birthday was turned into a national celebration. Each December the event was marked with parades of marching troops and happy children and workers. Again, the purpose of the cult was to allow ordinary citizens to identify with the regime by worshipping the leader. In this way, dissatisfaction with local conditions and economic hardship could be blamed on regional leaders while the good things in life were associated directly with Stalin.

'Long live the Stalinist Order of Heroes and Stakhanovites' by Gustavs Klucis

The Stalin cult changed significantly during Stalin's last years. First, it stressed his role as a war leader. From 1941 to 1945, Stalin led Russia in a battle against Germany. His success in the war was a continual theme in propaganda from then on. Secondly, following the Second World War, Stalin was presented as a world leader. In the mid-1940s, following the USSR's victory in the Second World War, much of Eastern Europe came under Russian control. The Soviet media credited Stalin with this success. Finally, towards the end of his life, Stalin attempted to establish a reputation for himself as an intellectual. In order to achieve this, he published an article about the theory of language, entitled 'Marxism and Problems of Linguistics'. The article appeared in 1950 and was praised in the Soviet press, where it was described as an intellectual breakthrough.

The 'cult of impersonality'

Stalin's biographer, Robert Service, has suggested that the Stalin cult is best understood as a 'cult of impersonality'. He argues that in spite of the continual worship of the vozhd, very little about Stalin's history and character was revealed to the Soviet people. Rather, Stalin deliberately kept his personal life extremely private. For example, prior to 1936, there was no mention in the official Soviet press of Stalin's children or family life. Indeed, for much of the 1930s, Stalin discouraged the publication of his early speeches and any attempts to write official biographies.

Rather than focusing on Stalin's personality, the Stalin cult centred on the glamorous or appealing side of the Soviet regime. For example, Stalin was often photographed with air force heroes, Stakhanovites and Russian explorers who had returned from their trips to the North and South Poles. In this way, the Stalin cult focused on the achievements of the regime rather than on Stalin as an individual.

Taking it further

1. Search the internet for Russian Socialist Realist images (you could try typing 'Russian Socialist Realism' into a search engine image search). These could be paintings, posters, photographs or sculptures.
2. Choose five contrasting images.
3. Print out these images, or import them into an electronic document.
4. Make notes around the images to highlight the key features of Socialist Realism and/or the cult of personality.
5. Try to remember these images when you are revising for your exam – they could be useful examples for your essays!

Conclusion

Stalin's totalitarian regime was built on fear, but not fear alone. During the famine and the Terror and the hardships of the Five-Year Plans, Soviet art offered the people a vision of a new society designed to inspire them to continue the struggle of building socialism. The leadership cults gave the impersonal Soviet bureaucracy a human face, and created a point of emotional contact between the regime and the people. Stalin's art allowed Soviet citizens to escape from the frustrations of everyday life, but in a way that tied them more closely to the regime. In this sense, Socialist Realism was as much a form of social control as the Great Terror.

Activity: The International Symposium on Socialist Realism in Stalin's Russia

You have been invited to participate in the *International Symposium* (an academic conference) *on Socialist Realism in Stalin's Russia.* As an expert in the field, you have been asked to present a paper (an academic lecture) on an aspect of Socialist Realism.

In small groups, you must prepare a short paper on one of the following topics:

- Painting
- Architecture
- Sculpture
- The cult of Lenin
- The cult of Stalin.

The symposium rules specify that your paper must be structured in the following way:

1. A short introduction, explaining the key features of the topic that you are presenting – specifying how this developed or changed under Stalin's leadership.

2. Three specific examples, to be shown as PowerPoint slides, and you must explain how each example illustrates the general points made in your introduction.

3. A conclusion, explaining how Stalin used this form of art to extend his control over Russia.

As you are presenting, your audience should make a record of your research – it may prove useful to them in the future. They should use the following template to record your key points and examples:

Title of paper:	
Key points from the introduction:	
Specific example 1 (name)	Details:
Specific example 2 (name)	Details:
Specific example 3 (name)	Details:
How did Stalin use this form of art to extend his control over Russia?	

At the end of the symposium you will be an expert on Stalinist culture!

Skills Builder 3: **Writing introductions and conclusions**

When answering questions in Unit 1, students will be expected to write an essay. So far, in Skills Builder 1, you have learned the importance of writing in paragraphs and, in Skills Builder 2, you have learned about the importance of showing a clear argument when answering questions on causation and change.

In this third Skills Builder, we will be looking at the importance of writing introductory and concluding paragraphs.

In your essay you will be answering a specific question. Your answer must be:

) Directly relevant to the question.

) Supported by relevant historical information.

) In the form of an argument which provides a historical analysis of the question.

When writing under examination conditions you should spend approximately 40 minutes on the whole of your essay. During this time you must:

) Plan what you are going to write.

) Write a separate paragraph for each major point you wish to make.

) Check through what you have written.

Therefore, given the time constraints, you should not spend more than 5 minutes writing your introduction.

What should you put in your introduction?

Your introduction should answer the question directly and set out what you plan to cover and discuss in your essay. Your introduction needs to show that you will answer the question in an analytical way – and that you haven't just started writing without thinking. Therefore, it is good to say, very briefly, what you are going to argue in the essay. You can then refer back to your introduction as you write, to make sure that your argument is on track.

We are going to look at an introduction to an answer to the following question:

> (A) How far do you agree that Stalin's paranoia was the main cause of the Great Terror?

This question gives one of the reasons for the Great Terror, and it asks you 'how far' you agree that it was the most important reason. This will require you to assess other reasons why the Terror occurred and make judgements about the significance of each reason in bringing about the Terror.

Here is an example of an introduction that you might write:

Stalin's paranoia was certainly one of the reasons for the Great Terror. However, it cannot be described as the main reason because this overlooks the significance of the murder of Kirov in 1934. Although many factors contributed to the outbreak of Terror – for example, the Congress of Victors, economic problems and Stalin's paranoia – it was the murder of Kirov that provided the trigger for the events that followed. Stalin used Kirov's murder to justify attacking his own Party and extending the role of the secret police.

This introduction answers the question directly. It recognises that the Great Terror had a number of causes, it states these causes, and it briefly explains which factor was most important and why.

Activity: Spot the mistake

The following introductions have been written in response to Question (A). Each one illustrates a common mistake. Spot them!

Example 1

There were many factors that caused the Great Terror. Stalin's paranoia was one, but there were also others. Some historians argue that the Great Terror was indeed caused by Stalin's paranoia. Other people say that it was the economy, the Congress of Victors, or Kirov's murder that caused the Terror of the 1930s. This essay will consider all of these factors.

Example 2

The Great Terror was an awful time for Russia and its citizens. It began in 1934 with the murder of Kirov. After this, Stalin turned his attention to the Leningrad Party, who he accused of murdering Kirov and plotting to murder himself. However, this was not the end of the Great Terror. As time went by, the Great Terror was extended and the Party outside Leningrad was also affected. Industrial managers, former opposition politicians and ethnic minorities were all victims of Stalin's Great Terror. Even Yezhov himself became a victim.

Example 3

Stalin's paranoia was the major cause of the Great Terror. He had been paranoid for a long time because everyone knew he was not as smart as Trotsky or Bukharin, he was not as close to Lenin as Zinoviev and Kamenev. He was really only an administrator, who many thought had become leader of Russia by accident. He feared that everyone was against him, and therefore he started the Great Terror, in which no one was safe because he trusted no one.

Example 3 – this introduction considers only one possible factor and therefore is highly unbalanced and does not show a range of knowledge.

Example 2 – this introduction tells the story of the Great Terror without answering the question.

Example 1 – this introduction considers a range of factors, but does not reach a judgement and therefore does not answer the question.

Answers

Activity: Write your own paragraph

It is important to link each of your paragraphs to the introduction. So, for Question (A), you could provide evidence in Paragraph 2 that explains the importance of Stalin's paranoia. Then, in Paragraph 3, you could explain why Kirov's murder was the most important cause of the Great Terror. In subsequent paragraphs you could explain the role played by the other relevant factors, such as the Congress of Victors and economic problems. It is important that your essay does not contradict your introduction. If you state in your introduction that Kirov's murder was the most important factor, then you must maintain this argument throughout your essay.

Introductions: DOs and DON'Ts

- DO look at the question and decide on your line of argument.

- DO make reference to the question in your introduction.

- DO show what you intend to argue.

- DON'T begin your answer by writing a story.

- DON'T spend too long writing your introduction. 5 minutes is enough.

Activity: Write your own introduction

Write an introduction to the following question:

> (B) How far do you agree that Socialist Realism was Stalin's
> most important method of social control?

You will need to draw on your knowledge of changes in industry and agriculture, social policy and the Great Terror, as well as Soviet art, in order to plan your introduction.

Why are conclusions important?

When you are asked a question in an examination, you are expected to answer it! The concluding paragraph is very important in this process. It should contain the summary of the argument you have made, with your *verdict* on the question.

Like an introduction, the conclusion should not be more than three or four sentences in length, and under examination conditions it should take no more than 5 minutes to write. Here is an example of a conclusion for Question (A):

The Great Terror was a result of a range of factors, such as the failure of Stalin's economic policy, his paranoia, the Congress of Victors, and Kirov's murder. However, the main reason for the outbreak of Terror was Kirov's murder rather than Stalin's paranoia. Stalin needed to divert people's attention from the failure of his economic policy, while the vote at the Congress of Victors fed his paranoia, which had been a feature of his personality for many years. However, without the murder of Kirov he would have been unable to persuade the Party and the public of the need for further repression. For this reason, the murder of Kirov can be seen as the main cause of the Great Terror.

Activity: Write your own conclusion

Using Question (B) above, about Socialist Realism, write a conclusion of not more than four sentences. Try to write it in 5 minutes.

Activity: Write an introduction and conclusion

Here is another example of a question:

> (C) How far do you agree that the main consequence of the
> Great Terror was the removal of Stalin's rivals?

Now write an introduction and a conclusion – each in approximately 5 minutes.

Tip – plan the conclusion first. You will always find it easier to write an introduction once you have decided what your conclusion will be. This is because once you know where your answer is going, you can introduce it.

Chapter 14 The Führer and the vozhd

Key questions

- Why did Stalin believe Russia should prepare for war?
- How effectively did Stalin prepare Russia for war?
- Why did Stalin sign the Nazi–Soviet Pact in 1939?

The British historian Sir Basil Liddell Hart once observed that 'Hitler was the only person Joseph Stalin ever trusted'. If this is true, then it is remarkable. First, Stalin's doctrine of 'socialism in one country' had emphasised Russia's isolation from the rest of the world. Secondly, it is remarkable because Stalin's paranoia was well known – he literally trusted no one. Thirdly, Hitler had publicly stated that he hated Communism and planned to invade Russia to destroy Germany's mortal enemy. Fourthly, it is remarkable because Stalin's trust was so misplaced. Having executed thousands of people who posed little threat to him, Stalin was betrayed by the one man he thought he understood.

Take note

1. Copy the timeline.
2. As you read through this chapter, add details to the events mentioned on the timeline.
3. Your notes on the events from 1935 to 1940 should describe the process of Stalin's preparation for war. Divide these notes to illustrate the stages by which Stalin prepared for war. In order to do this, consider how his priorities and focus changed over time.

Preparing for war

Since the late 1920s, the Soviet Union had believed that Germany was preparing for war. Concern about war intensified with the appointment of Hitler as German Chancellor in 1933 and the agreement of a treaty between Nazi Germany, Fascist Italy and Imperial Japan that explicitly recognised Communism as a common enemy. For this reason, the Soviet government reformed the military, recruited spies and started to divert economic resources towards rearmament. However, these measures were not as effective as they could have been. In each case, Stalin's paranoia undermined efforts to prepare effectively.

Timeline

1933	Adolf Hitler becomes Chancellor of Germany
1935	Military discipline tightened in the Red Army
1937–1938	Purge of the Red Army
1938	Third Five-Year Plan launched
1939	Nazi-Soviet Pact Hitler invades Poland Red Army attacks Finland
1940	Stalin overthrows the governments of Estonia, Latvia and Lithuania
1941	Germany invades the USSR

Reforming the military

In 1935, in preparation for war, military discipline within the Red Army was tightened. Under Trotsky, titles such as officer had been abolished, and commanders and regular soldiers were encouraged to treat each other as comrades. However, under Stalin, the old Tsarist system of strict discipline and a clear division between officers and men was reintroduced. Additionally, between 1937 and 1938, the Red Army was extensively purged to try to ensure that all of its members were loyal to the regime. Consequently, a great deal of experience and military skill was lost.

International espionage

Russia had a huge advantage over other foreign powers because of its extensive network of spies. Communist sympathisers at all levels of the government in the United Kingdom, USA, France and Germany provided secret information willingly to the Soviet government. However, much of this information was never analysed, as Stalin refused to trust his intelligence service and, as for much of the 1930s, Russia's intelligence resources were focused on the hunt for Trotsky, leaving little capacity for monitoring foreign enemies.

Economic preparation

In theory, rearmament was an essential part of the Third Five-Year Plan. However, the purges led to chaos in major government departments, and as a result the Plan was never completed – and, in fact, never published. Administrators were forced to work from drafts of the Plan which included little detail about how rearmament was to be achieved. Additionally, there was no agreed budget for military spending, and seventeen different government departments argued with Gosplan over the amount of money to be allocated to war production. Broadly, it is estimated that during the Third Five-Year Plan, the Soviet government spent over eleven times more on defence than under the First Five-Year Plan (see table).

In spite of the chaotic nature of the Third Five-Year Plan, Soviet industry achieved some remarkable feats. For example, in 1939, six new aircraft factories were built, as well as twenty-four new factories dedicated to the production of explosives. In addition, the total number of tanks produced in 1942 was twice that produced in 1938.

Russian war preparation compared favourably with that of the Germans (see table overleaf). Germany spent more on preparation for war from 1935 to 1940. But, on the eve of war, Russia was able to overtake German military spending. This is because the Russian economy was more powerful than that of Germany. For example, the $5 billion that Russia spent on its military in 1940 represented only 20 per cent of its national income. In contrast, the $6 billion that Germany spent on its military represented 44 per cent of its national income. Clearly, Russia had much more scope to expand military production than Germany.

The Nazi–Soviet Pact

Military preparation was not the government's only strategy for ensuring national security. Stalin was also prepared to negotiate with Germany, his sworn enemy, in a bid to protect Russia.

Glossary: Führer

German for 'leader'. The term was used in Germany between 1933 and 1945 to refer to Adolf Hitler. Hitler preferred to be described as Führer rather than President or Chancellor because the title implied that his power was not based on his official position and therefore it was unlimited. In many ways, the German term 'Führer' is similar to the Russian term 'vozhd'.

Rearmament: production in 1938 and targets for 1943

	1938	Target for 1943
Aircraft	20,500	50,000
Tanks	35,400	125,000
Machine guns	250,000	450,000
Chemical weapons (tonnes)	122,000	298,000
Explosives (tonnes)	280,000	1,035,000

Estimated figures for defence spending (roubles)

First Five-Year Plan	Second Five-Year Plan	Third Five-Year Plan
366 million	2080 million	4200 million

Take note

As you read through the next section, answer the questions below, using fewer than 50 words for each answer.
1. Why was the Pact between Stalin and Hitler a 'surprising alliance'?
2. What was specified in (a) the public, and (b) the secret sections of the Pact?
3. Why did Stalin agree to sign the Nazi–Soviet Pact, even though he expected Hitler to break the agreement?

Russian and German defence spending (billions of US dollars)

	1935–1939	1940	1941
USSR	1.6	5	8.5
Germany	2.4	6	6

Fascism

Fascism is a political ideology and a style of government. As an ideology, it suggests that human beings are essentially irrational. Therefore, they are incapable of self-government and need a strong leader. Secondly, it suggests that human beings are unequal and that some are naturally superior. Fascist ideology is also associated with nationalism, and in many cases, racism. Finally, fascism suggests that war is a natural and virtuous activity that encourages humans to be noble. In terms of government, fascism tends towards a one-party dictatorship. It also attempts to control the economy in order to create a war economy. For all of these reasons fascist regimes have been described as totalitarian. The German Nazis have often been described as fascist.

A surprising alliance

In many ways, an alliance between Stalin and Hitler seemed unthinkable. Hitler's autobiography, *Mein Kampf* (1925), bitterly attacked Soviet communism and proposed invading Russia in order to acquire 'living space' for his 'master race'. Equally, the Communist Party had described Nazism as one of the worst regimes of the age. Finally, Russian and German soldiers had fought each other during the Spanish Civil War of 1936–1939. Clearly Stalin and Hitler were unlikely bedfellows.

The Pact

In spite of the official hatred between the two regimes, the Nazi–Soviet Pact was negotiated in little over three hours on 24 August 1939. The Pact had two sections, one of which was published. The other remained secret. Publicly, Russia and Germany agreed to respect each other's territories, to settle any disagreements through negotiation and to increase trade as a sign of friendship. Privately, the Pact divided Eastern Europe into two 'spheres of interest'. Germany was to control western Poland and Czechoslovakia, whilst Russia was free to pursue its own policies in Latvia, Lithuania and Estonia. Stalin was apparently so pleased to sign the Pact that he shook with excitement during the ceremony. A week later, German troops entered Poland and, within a month, they had captured the Polish capital. In the spirit of the agreement, Stalin telegraphed Hitler to congratulate him.

Stalin's decision

Stalin alone was responsible for Russia's pact with Hitler. Indeed, the Russian Foreign Office played no part in the negotiations. Stalin had many reasons for dealing with Hitler. First, there were no viable alternatives. Neither France nor the United Kingdom seemed interested in an alliance with Russia. Secondly, it has been argued by Robert Service that Stalin was attempting to 'buy time' before starting a war with Hitler. Service argues that Stalin was aware that the Red Army would not be ready for war until 1943 and therefore the Pact was a bid to delay an inevitable conflict. Thirdly, Stalin was following Lenin's example. In 1920, Lenin had advised German communists to form an alliance with German fascists in order to overthrow the democratic government. Fourthly, Stalin admired Hitler. He regarded him as a strong and decisive leader and believed that he enjoyed great support from the German people. Finally, Stalin was keen to recapture European territory that had once belonged to the Tsar. Indeed, within a month of signing the treaty, Stalin had overthrown the governments of Estonia, Latvia and Lithuania, and, during the winter of 1940, the Red Army attacked Finland.

Stalin believed that Hitler would break the terms of the Nazi–Soviet Pact and invade Russia. However, Hitler's military success gave Stalin good reason for honouring the terms of the treaty. The German Army had effectively conquered Poland in less than a month. By mid-1940, Hitler had also overrun France and Holland, and forced British soldiers to flee continental Europe. By contrast, the Red Army had performed abysmally. The invasion of Finland had been a failure and had shown the world how Stalin's purges had destroyed the Russian army. With this in mind, Stalin was keen to delay a confrontation with Hitler for as long as possible. He believed the Pact would ensure that Russia had nothing to fear before May 1942.

Conclusion

Stalin was wrong. Germany invaded Russia at 4 a.m. on Sunday, 22 June 1941. Russia, despite having some of the best intelligence in the world, was unprepared. Stalin's chaotic economic preparation, the purging of the army and the misuse of espionage ensured that this invasion would have disastrous consequences for the people of Russia. Nonetheless, in spite of Stalin's phenomenal failings, the national crisis united the people of Russia behind their vozhd.

Activity: Stalin exposed!

1. In the centre of a large piece of paper, write the following question: 'Why was Stalin unprepared for war?'

2. Around the edge of this question, write the following factors: 'Economic preparation', 'Military preparation', 'Espionage' and 'Relationship with Hitler'.

3. Around the edge of the piece of paper, write the following topics: 'Stalin's rise to power', 'Economic policy' and 'The Terror State'. Your piece of paper should look like this:

4. The factors around the question explain why Stalin was unprepared for war. The topics around the edge of the paper represent the background to the outbreak of war. Draw links between the factors and the topics to illustrate the ways in which Stalin's policies and experiences led to the Soviet Union's lack of preparation for war.

5. On your diagram, explain these links. An example is shown below:

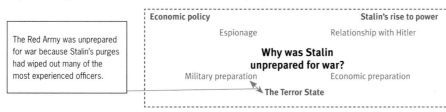

6. It is July 1941, and Germany has just invaded Russia. The Red Army has been shown to be completely unprepared for the task of repelling Hitler. Put yourself in the position of a Trotskyist in exile. Using the diagram you have just drawn, write a propaganda bulletin (or create a propaganda poster) exposing Stalin's role in this military catastrophe.

   In your report, make sure that you state which factor you feel was most significant in Russia's lack of preparation for war. Explain why you think this is the most significant factor.

Chapter 15 The course and cost of the war

Key questions

- What were the stages of Russia's defeat of Germany in the Second World War?
- What was the human cost of Russia's involvement in the Second World War?
- What was the economic cost of Russia's involvement in the Second World War?

The Nazis invented a whole new type of warfare. Blitzkrieg, literally meaning 'lightning war', revolutionised warfare in the twentieth century. Hitler's idea was to deploy massive military strength, including colossal air power, highly trained infantry and tank battalions, in a coordinated and fast-moving assault. Hitler's Blitzkrieg against Russia in 1941 and 1942 met little effective resistance, and Russia's defeat in these years was greater than in any war in its history. But while the defeat was enormous, the victory that the Russian army won in 1944 and 1945 was equally historic. Indeed, by May 1945, the Red Army had planted the Red Flag in the centre of Berlin, achieving a victory that far surpassed Hitler's early successes. Nonetheless, victory came at a high price for Russia's people and economy.

Take note

As you read through this section, compile a timeline of the key events of Russia's involvement in World War Two.

Blitzkrieg

Hitler had always intended to invade Russia. By mid-1941, the German army were well prepared for war with Russia – and they appeared invincible. In June, Hitler, convinced of his own strength, launched Operation Barbarossa – 'Operation Red Beard' – an all-out attack on the Soviet Union, focusing primarily on the cities of Moscow and Stalingrad.

Operation Typhoon

In September 1941, Operation Typhoon was launched to capture Moscow. Under threat of invasion, the people of Moscow panicked, and rioting and looting broke out in the city. Law and order broke down, government buildings were deserted, and it was rumoured that Stalin was already in German hands. By December, General Zhukov had launched the first Russian counter-attack, which successfully pushed the German army back to about 200 kilometres from the centre of Moscow.

Operation Blue

Hitler's Operation Blue was launched in June 1942 and aimed to capture the city of Stalingrad. Hitler believed that if he could overrun Stalingrad, he would deprive the Russian war effort of a vital industrial base, and score an enormous propaganda victory by conquering the city that bore Stalin's name. The six-month Battle of Stalingrad, beginning in August 1942, was arguably the bloodiest in human history. At one point during the battle, it was estimated that the life expectancy of a Russian soldier there was less than 24 hours. Officers fared better, lasting around three days. Over 1.9 million people died during the siege, but still the Russians resisted.

Stalin to blame?

The appalling losses suffered by the Russian people in 1941 and 1942 were the result, in large part, of Stalin's mismanagement of the Russian military. He had precise information from British intelligence, as well as Russian spies, regarding the timing of the attack. Nonetheless, he refused to believe it. This was not Stalin's only failing. The army purges had significantly weakened the Russian military. Additionally, Stalin ignored the advice of leading Red Army generals who were keen to update the Russian military strategy. War planning was confused, chaotic and limited by the purges of Gosplan. The officers and planners who survived the purges did so by emphasising the 'invincibility' of the Red Army. Essentially, they told Stalin what he wanted to hear, and in so doing, concealed the many shortcomings of the Russian military.

Counter-attack

Stalin was determined not to lose Moscow, Leningrad or Stalingrad. The Soviet slogan during these battles was 'Not a step back!' Stalin mobilised the entire resources of the Soviet Union for war. In Stalingrad, for example, the initial defence of the city was conducted, in the main, by women volunteers.

Operation Uranus

The Soviet counter-offensive, Operation Uranus, was launched in September 1942. The defence of Stalingrad alone cost 1.1 million Red Army lives, and 800,000 German troops were killed during the conflict. But by February 1943, the Germans had been driven from Stalingrad, and by December 1943, two-thirds of the German-occupied territory had been recaptured. Early in 1944, Soviet propaganda proclaimed 'Ten Great Victories', which included the recapture of the Crimea, Belarus, Latvia and Estonia.

Germany

By early January 1945, the Red Army had entered German territory, and Russian soldiers sought revenge for the Nazi invasion. There are numerous accounts of atrocities such as rape and murder perpetrated by the advancing Red Army on the first Germans they encountered. Western historian Marius Broekmeyer states 'There was no end to the destruction. Towns and villages that had fallen virtually unscathed into the hands of the Russians were subsequently reduced to ashes by Red Army units.'

Berlin

By April 1945, some 4,000 Red Army tanks, 23,000 pieces of artillery and 4,000 aeroplanes had reached the outskirts of Berlin, and in May 1945, Germany surrendered to the Western allies and USSR. In homage to his homeland, Stalin ordered that a Georgian soldier should be given the honour of planting the Red Flag on top of the German Parliament building.

The human cost of the war

The exact number of Russian deaths caused by the Second World War is disputed. Nonetheless, at least 10 per cent of Russia's population died

Take note

1. Using the next two sections, make notes on the human and economic impact of the Second World War on Russia. The notes can be in any form you wish, but remember that the purpose of note-taking is to capture important information in a clear and organised way.
2. In pairs, swap notes. Assess your peer's notes in terms of
   (a) their organisation,
   (b) their clarity and
   (c) their choice of material.
3. List two ways in which your peer could improve their note-taking skills.
4. List two ways in which you have learned from your peer's notes.

between 1941 and 1945, and conservative estimates suggest that 20 million Russian citizens died as a result of the conflict. However, when the numbers who died in gulags or died from war-related injuries are included, the figure rises to more than 30 million. The war also caused social upheaval of other kinds. For example, 85 million Russians (approximately 45 per cent of the Soviet population) were under German control for much of the war. Additionally, 20 million Russians fled west at the end of the war, in order to escape Communist repression. Some of the other population movements were directly ordered by Stalin. As already noted, the Kalmyk people were moved from the Stalingrad and Rostov provinces in western Russia to Siberia, in order to prevent collaboration with the Germans. Approximately 130,000 Kalmyks were forcibly relocated in this way, but because of the brutal treatment they received – and Siberia's harsh conditions – 60 per cent of them died in the following years.

Working through the war

Working conditions were already poor before the outbreak of the war. In agriculture especially, they deteriorated further during the conflict. For example, the production and maintenance of tractors effectively ceased because factories were converted for the production of tanks and aircraft . As a result, fields were ploughed by hand. Workers in farms and factories were expected to work seven days a week for the entire duration of the war. Factory shifts lasted between 12 and 18 hours. On top of this, factory workers were expected to work an additional night shift on farms during the harvest season. The first day off in four years was 9 May 1945.

Discipline in factories was tightened further during the war. Workers who were twenty minutes late or who were caught stealing were handed over to the military and tried for their crimes. Workers who changed jobs without the appropriate authorisation faced between five and eight years' imprisonment.

Women at war

It has been argued that Russian women bore the brunt of the Russian war effort. They were expected to work in factories and fields, whilst at the same time caring for their families. What is more, they had to cope with the continual shortages and hunger which were an everyday reality during the war. Women made up the majority of the Russian workforce during the war. Indeed, in some regions, such as Shadrinsk, they made up 75 per cent of the workforce. Women were also frequently required to perform tasks that were usually performed by machines or animals. For example, in many areas, women were yoked to ploughs in the absence of tractors and horses.

Family at war

The war affected all groups within Russian society. The family was no exception. Young people between the ages of 14 and 17 were generally drafted into 'labour reserve schools', a form of vocational training in preparation for war work. Families were also disrupted in a second sense. Senior Party members, usually from Leningrad or Moscow, were sent to regional factories or collective farms in order to organise production. As they

Source 15.1: A.P. Pustynnykh, who worked at the SAAZ factory, describes conditions in 1943

The working conditions were really bad. We had poor food, usually nettle soup for lunch containing nothing more than finely chopped nettles (not even any potato). The people were tired; they often fell asleep in the production hall or on the toilet. That led to a lot of accidents. Fatigue breaks you, you doze off, and your hair gets caught in the workbench. But worse things happened. Zina Shurulchik, for example, was scalped; the hair was pulled off her head along with her scalp; she was in hospital for a long time, but she recovered.

Taken from: *Stalin, the Russians and their War* by Marius Broekmeyer (2004)

worked away from home for a period of years, it was common for them to start a second family. At the end of the war, many deserted their so-called 'war family' to return home.

The economic cost of the war

The Soviet authorities claimed that the Second World War set back the economy by ten years. Indeed, western economic analysts argue that the Second World War effectively wiped out the economic progress made during the first two Five-Year Plans.

Production and consumption

The German forces quickly occupied a large part of Russian territory, and by January 1942, they had gained control of one-third of Russia's industry and agriculture. At the same time, Russian labour was being conscripted into the armed forces. Both of these facts led to a significant downturn in economic production during the war. In 1942, Russia's industry was producing only 59 per cent of its 1940 output. Due to a heroic effort, this figure rose to 79 per cent in 1944. Grain production was also affected, with production in 1942 only 36 per cent of that in 1940. Again, by 1944, the situation had improved to 64 per cent. In both cases, in spite of tremendous hard work, production still lagged behind the pre-war figures.

In terms of consumption, living standards significantly diminished. Electricity supplies to the general population were ended late in 1941, and were restored only once the war was over. Workers were sustained by meagre rations, while the government took 90 per cent of the produce of collective farms. For the Russian population under siege in Leningrad, Moscow and Stalingrad, conditions were worse still. In Leningrad, for example, the population were sustained on little more than 'blockade bread', made largely from sawdust. Citizens were also sustained by eating birds, rats, their pets, and – in extreme cases – by resorting to cannibalism.

Infrastructure

In June 1941, the Sovnarkom decreed that workers should destroy or sabotage all industrial equipment that was likely to fall into German hands. The Germans adopted a similar policy following 1943, when they were forced to retreat. It is estimated that a quarter of Russia's pre-war industrial equipment was destroyed between 1941 and 1945. In areas occupied by German forces, more than two-thirds of industrial equipment was destroyed. In retreat, the German army operated a scorched-earth policy. In order to prevent the Russians gaining economically from their military success, the German army burned crops, destroyed factories and machinery, killed cattle and blew up bridges. Overall, it is believed that 70,000 villages, 32,000 factories and 65,000 km of railway were destroyed as a result of the war.

Conclusion

The Soviet victory of 2 May 1945 represented a heroic achievement for Stalin and the people of Russia. Many in the West had believed that Russia would

be overrun by German forces by the end of 1942. The fact that they had survived – and the fact of their victory – was in many ways miraculous. But this miracle had come at great cost. Russia, her people and her economy had been shattered. Stalin had pushed his people to the limit. The hard work and malnutrition he inflicted on his people had led to almost as many deaths as the German invasion itself. In winning, Stalin had gained a tremendous prize. He was now one of the most powerful men in the world and master of an emerging superpower whose influence extended from East Asia to Berlin.

Activity: Stalinism under fire!

Taking it further

At the Victory Parade on 24 June 1945, Stalin gave a speech in which he referred to the 'simple, ordinary, modest people, the "little cogs" who keep our great state mechanism in an active condition'. The historian Robert Service comments that 'the "people" for him [Stalin] were mere cogs in the machinery of state, and not individuals. The state took precedence over society.' Using your knowledge of the Russian war effort, and your knowledge of Soviet Russia as a whole, how far do you agree with Robert Service that Stalin treated the people like tiny cogs who served his great government machine?

1. On small cards, briefly record the social and economic policies introduced during the Second World War. This means any official initiative by the Soviet government. Record one factor on each small card.

2. Divide your small cards into two piles. In the first pile, place the cards which you believe show that Stalin's policies during the war were a continuation of his pre-war policies. In the second pile, place the cards which show that Stalin changed his policies during the war.

3. Stick each pile of cards on to a large sheet of paper. Annotate the cards to show how these policies illustrate continuities and changes.

4. Use your cards and annotations to write a short essay in answer to the question: 'How far was Soviet social and economic policy during the Second World War a continuation of pre-war policy?' Structure your essay as follows:

   ◗ Introduction

   ◗ Evidence of continuity

   ◗ Evidence of change

   ◗ Conclusion.

Chapter 16 **Why Russia won**

Key questions

⦾ How far was the Soviet economy responsible for Russia's victory in the Second World War?
⦾ What methods did Stalin use to boost morale in Russia during the war?
⦾ To what extent did the Second World War expose the weaknesses in Stalin's Communist system?

The foundations of Russia's victory in the Second World War were laid in the 1930s. It was during these years that Russian industrialised and developed economic planning techniques. It was also during the 1930s that the American company Hormel Foods Corporation launched SPAM, a canned meat product. SPAM's role in Russia's victory is often overlooked. Nonetheless, Nikita Khrushchev, the Soviet leader who succeeded Stalin, was in no doubt: 'without SPAM', he once said, 'we should not have been able to feed our army'. American assistance, particularly the provision of foodstuffs such as SPAM, was one of the essential ingredients which, along with the Soviet economy and sacrifices on the Home Front, ensured the Allied victory.

Russia's war economy

Soviet economic preparation for the Second World War was imperfect. However, when Russia entered the war, it was better prepared than either Britain or France in the same situation. This was largely a result of the economic progress made during the first two Five-Year Plans. The Soviet economy also compared favourably with the Nazi system, which was unable to produce armaments on the scale necessary to defeat Russia, and unable to capitalise on the resources won through conquest.

Gosplan at war

The Soviet economy used similar methods to fight the war as it had under the Five-Year Plans. There were, however, some innovations. For example, in the early days of the war, Stalin initiated a new policy of relocating industry to the east in order to stop it falling into enemy hands. Indeed, by November 1941, 1,523 factories had been taken apart and reassembled in Russia's eastern regions. Central planning was highly effective during the Second World War. By 1942, 56 per cent of Russia's national income was devoted to the war. This was a much higher figure than in Britain, Germany or America. The production of armaments almost doubled between 1941 and 1944. This was a remarkable achievement, given the fact that, for this entire period, a great deal of Russian territory and industry was in German hands.

The Nazi war economy

In theory, the Nazis had been preparing for war since 1933. In practice, however, the Nazi economy lacked direction. Senior Nazis had a series of competing priorities which hampered the effective preparation for war. For

Take note

1. As you read through this chapter, make a detailed list of all the reasons why Russia won the Second World War.
2. Copy the Venn diagram below.

3. Plot the reasons from your list on to the Venn diagram, to show who was responsible for each. For example, the Lend-Lease scheme could be placed in the section shared by the USSR and the Allies.
4. How far was Russia responsible for its victory in the Second World War?

example, Hitler and the Nazi economic boss, Hermann Goering, insisted that living standards should be kept high in order to ensure popular support. Additionally, Goering made a number of mistakes which hampered war production. For example, he opposed the introduction of mass production in the German aircraft industry. Consequently, for much of the war, Germany produced fewer than 1,000 aircraft a month. Therefore, by 1943, Hitler reckoned that the German economy was four years behind schedule.

German tactical mistakes

In the early part of the Second World War, Germany looked unstoppable. Nonetheless, as Hitler's self-confidence grew, his ability to guide the war effectively proved to be inadequate. First, launching a war against Russia whilst still fighting Britain was over-ambitious. Indeed, Operation Barbarossa was launched later than German strategists had anticipated. For this reason, the German army was unable to reach Moscow before the first snows of winter, and found themselves unprepared for the harsh conditions. Secondly, Hitler decided to lay siege to Leningrad and Moscow, rather than taking them by force. This prolonged the war and gave the Russian armed forces time to regroup and mount a successful counter-offensive. Finally, Hitler sent troops to Stalingrad and Ukraine before conquering Leningrad or Moscow. This move overstretched the German army and meant that Hitler was unable to conquer Russia's capital.

The Home Front

An essential factor in the Soviet war victory was the effective mobilisation of the Russian population on the Home Front. Stalin was under no illusions – the Russians were 'fighting for their homeland, not for the Communists'. Socialism would not motivate the people to fight, and therefore Stalin turned to traditional nationalism and the Russian Orthodox Church in order to mobilise his people.

The Great Patriotic War

Stalin realised that the Russian people had little reason to fight to preserve the Soviet system. The Soviet economy had done little to improve living standards, and the Great Terror had affected the vast majority of Russia's citizens. Consequently, Stalin did not appeal to the Russian people in the name of socialism. Rather, he called on the Russian people to defend the '**Motherland**'. The war was named the 'Great Patriotic War'. In the army, soldiers were encouraged to use nationalistic nicknames, such as 'Fritz', 'Hans' and 'Kraut', to refer to the Germans. This emphasised the fact that the Germans were a foreign enemy rather than an ideological one.

Stalin's appeal to patriotism evidently stirred the Russian people. In many ways, the Great Patriotic War is a story of the endurance and resistance of the Russian people. The citizens of Leningrad, for example, endured a German siege for nine hundred days, but never surrendered in spite of starvation, exhaustion and severe Russian winters. Following the war, the city was awarded the title 'Hero City' by Stalin in recognition of its valour.

Glossary:
Motherland

A term used, predominantly by Russians, to describe their home country. It implies that the country nurtures its citizens, and that in response they owe their country loyalty, love and affection.

Turning to the Church

The Russian Orthodox Church had traditionally been an important part of Russian national identity. With the reawakening of patriotism, it was natural for many Russians to look to the Church for guidance. Since 1917, the Communists had been extremely hostile to the Church. However, this changed with the onset of war. Anti-religious propaganda ceased from the outset of war. Indeed, the Communist publication *Bezbozhnik* ('The Godless'), was officially closed down during the first year of the war. Stalin granted Metropolitan Sergey (the Russian Orthodox Church's most senior figure) an official residence in Moscow, and promised that religious magazines would no longer be censored following the war. Metropolitan Sergey responded by stating that Stalin was 'God's chosen leader'. The government's tolerance of religion is also evident from the fact that 414 churches were allowed to reopen during the final year of the war. As one soldier commented, the words of Jesus were more comforting in the face of death than the works of Marx, Lenin and Stalin combined.

The Grand Alliance

Russia's victory against the Nazis cannot be entirely explained by the mobilisation of its economy and society. The Nazis were defeated by a Grand Alliance of the British Empire, the United States of America and the USSR. The Alliance brought together unprecedented military might and provided Russia with strategic economic support.

A marriage of convenience

From the end of 1941, Russia was in an informal alliance with the British and the United States. The alliance was based on the fact that all three countries faced a common enemy. Other than this, there was little that united Britain and America with the USSR. The western powers were capitalists, whereas Russia was Communist. Britain and America were democracies, whereas Stalin's Russia was a totalitarian dictatorship – not unlike Nazi Germany. The relationship between the three great powers was uneasy. Stalin continually protested that Britain and America were not doing enough to help the Russian war effort. Stalin demanded a British invasion of France in 1942 in order to divert the Nazis' attention from Russia. Winston Churchill, the British war leader, believed that Stalin's view of the war was highly unrealistic. Moreover, Churchill never trusted Stalin. Nonetheless, the British and the Russians signed a formal treaty in May 1942, and officially became allies against the Nazi menace. Franklin Roosevelt, the American President, naively believed that Stalin could be trusted and, in spite of American intelligence, felt that Stalin would work for 'a world of democracy and peace'.

Together, the Grand Alliance defeated the Nazis. From the first, the Alliance divided Hitler's attention and in so doing, lessened the threat to the Russian people. British bombers targeted German cities and therefore the German air force (the Luftwaffe) could not concentrate its attentions on Russia. What is more, following D-Day, the British and Americans opened a third front against Germany in France. In the final analysis, the Nazis could not withstand the combined forces of the Grand Alliance.

Lend-Lease

Roosevelt's trust in Stalin's good faith meant that he was prepared to offer Russia America's full assistance. 'Lend-Lease' was the scheme established by Roosevelt to supply the British with American resources to fight the Nazis. From November 1941, the scheme was extended to aid the Russian war effort. Nonetheless, in practice, Lend-Lease was of only minor significance in terms of military support. According to official Soviet figures, 12 per cent of the aeroplanes, 10 per cent of the tanks and 2 per cent of the artillery used by the Red Army during the Second World War were supplied by the Americans. Similarly, Lend-Lease was of little significance in terms of Russian industry. Gosplan estimated that, in total, Lend-Lease accounted for only 4 per cent of the industrial goods used during the Second World War.

Lend-Lease was of more significance in terms of food and transport. The Red Army was dependent on American and Canadian wheat and tinned goods such as SPAM. By 1943, approximately 17 per cent of the calorie intake of the Red Army was supplied by the Americans. By the end of the war, it was estimated that the 12 million soldiers in the Red Army were receiving about 200 grams of US food every day. Secondly, the Red Army was highly dependent on American-produced transport. For example, of the 2,000 trains used by the Russians during the Second World War, over 1,900 were American. Equally, American 'jeeps' – produced by Dodge and Studebaker – formed two-thirds of all those used by the Red Army.

Overall, in terms of food and transport, Lend-Lease was critical to Russian success. It was also important for providing specialist products, such as aluminium and high-quality steel. Nonetheless, in terms of the production of armaments, Lend-Lease was less significant. Finally, it is worth noting that Stalin was highly suspicious of Lend-Lease. His concern stemmed from the fact that American goods were clearly superior to those made by the Russians. In this sense, they proved the superiority of capitalist forms of production and revealed the inadequacies of Russia's planned economy. For this reason, the praise of foreign technology was officially criminalised in 1942.

Conclusion

The Second World War highlighted the inadequacies of the Soviet system: Stalin's communism could not count on the support of the Russian people, and Stalin was forced to turn to more traditional forces, such as nationalism and religion, to inspire the people. Additionally, socialist agriculture, which had been reformed by Stalin, proved inadequate without the help of capitalist nations. Only Soviet industry, against huge odds, was able to meet the needs of the war.

The war effort placed an enormous burden on Russia's people and infrastructure. As many as 10 per cent of Russia's population died during the war, employees of Soviet factories were expected to work double and triple shifts throughout the war, without a single day off, and the Soviet economy suffered billions of dollars' worth of damage. Stalin presented Russia's victory as a triumph for socialism. In reality, it was a triumph for Russia's people rather than for the regime under which they lived.

Activity: Dear Dmitri ...

Historians have disagreed about the reasons why Russia was able to defeat Germany in the Second World War. Soviet historians, for example, often played down the significance of the Lend-Lease scheme, preferring to concentrate on the success of Russia's economy. This trend has continued in post-Soviet Russian historiography. Dmitri Volkogonov's 600-page biography of Stalin, to take a case in point, makes no mention of Lend-Lease.

Imagine that it is 1991 – Volkogonov's biography of Stalin has just been published. Your task is to write a letter or report addressed to Volkogonov expressing one of two opinions: either you must agree with the author that Lend-Lease played no role in the Russian victory and explain the reasons for your agreement, or you must demonstrate why you believe that he is wrong.

1. First, in order to understand the relative significance of the different factors that contributed to Russian victory in the Second World War, complete the following table:

The significance of different factors in Russia's victory

Factor	Evidence that it played an important role	Evidence that it played a limited role
Russia's economy		
Russian Home Front		
Military factors (including German and Allied tactics)		
Lend-Lease		

2. Having completed this table, use the information to write a letter or report to send to Volkogonov. Your letter or report must be carefully structured to cover all factors that contributed to the Soviet victory, and must provide evidence to support your points. Make sure that your argument is clear throughout your writing – so that if Volkogonov only had time to read one paragraph, he would not be in any doubt about your opinion.

3. Conclude your letter or report with a clear statement of the extent to which you believe Lend-Lease was the crucial factor in the Russian victory over Germany. Ensure that this conclusion is supported by a brief summary of your argument.

Taking it further

This chapter has argued that the Second World War exposed weaknesses in Stalin's system. However, it is also possible to point to ways in which the Communist system facilitated Russia's war effort.

With this in mind, make two lists:
(a) Ways in which the Stalinist system hindered Russia's war effort, and
(b) Ways in which the Stalinist system boosted Russia's war effort.

Overall, do you believe that Stalinism aided or hindered the fight against Hitler?

Chapter 17 The new world order

Key questions

- In what ways was the Soviet Union a superpower by 1953?
- How did Russia's relationships with other countries change in the post-war world?
- In what ways had Stalin transformed Russia by 1953?

The Second World War had not merely changed Russia – it had changed the world. The age of empires was over, and the age of superpowers had just begun. Following 1945 the world was dominated by Russia and America, the two superpowers of the late twentieth century. Russia and America were superpowers by virtue of the fact that they controlled large parts of the earth's surface. Moreover, they were superpowers in the sense that their economies were the most powerful in the world. Finally, both superpowers had enormous military strength, and by 1950, both possessed the power of ultimate destruction – the nuclear bomb.

Take note

Copy the following diagram. Use this first section to add notes to your diagram, explaining the political reasons why the USSR was considered a superpower at this time.

> **Why was the USSR considered a superpower in the post-war world?**

Political factors

Timeline

1943	November: Tehran Conference
1944	December: Beria and the NKVD put in charge of the Soviet atomic bomb project
1945	February: Yalta Conference July/August: Potsdam Conference
1946	January: Fourth Five-Year Plan launched March: Winston Churchill's 'Iron Curtain' speech
1947	People's Democracies established in Poland and Hungary
1948	People's Democracies established in Czechoslovakia, Romania and Bulgaria
1949	People's Democracy established in East Germany August: First test of the Soviet atomic bomb
1953	March: Stalin's death

Global superpower

The alliance between Russia, America and Britain had never been an easy one. Indeed, even before the fall of Berlin, all sides were contemplating a continuation of the Second World War in which America and Britain would fight the USSR. By 1946, the Grand Alliance of the Second World War had broken down and, in Stalin's words, 'two camps' had emerged. Eastern Europe allied with the Soviet Union under the banner of socialism. Western Europe, together with the USA, followed a different course, embracing capitalism and democracy.

Spheres of influence

During the Second World War, the 'big three' – Stalin, Roosevelt, and Churchill – were already planning the post-war world. At conferences in Tehran and Yalta, it was agreed that once the Nazis were defeated, Europe

would be divided in two. Churchill and Roosevelt agreed that Russia could legitimately expect to have neighbouring states that were sympathetic to communism – within its 'sphere of influence'.

The Yalta Conference, in February 1945, agreed a joint 'Allied Declaration on Liberated Europe' which committed the victorious powers to establish democratic regimes in the territories that they occupied. However, Stalin's interpretation of a legitimate Soviet 'sphere of influence' had no room for western democracy. Consequently, Stalin ordered the Red Army to establish communist governments in Eastern Germany, Czechoslovakia, Hungary, Poland, Romania and Bulgaria. The Communist Parties in these areas were kept loyal to Russia through regular purges, orchestrated from Moscow.

Exporting Stalinism to eastern Europe

Stalin had established regimes called 'People's Democracies' throughout eastern Europe. Politically, they followed the Stalinist model. Regular elections allowed the people to vote for the Communist Party alone. At the top of each Communist Party stood a ruling Politburo, and in each new People's Democracy opposition was suppressed through a mix of terror and propaganda. The economies of eastern European countries were not fully Stalinist. Nonetheless, trade agreements were drawn up between Russia and other eastern European states which clearly favoured Russia. By 1949, an 'Eastern Bloc' had emerged. According to western commentators, countries in the Eastern Bloc were not truly independent. Rather, they were controlled from Moscow which forced them to act in such a way as to bring maximum benefit to the USSR.

Cold War

In February 1946, Stalin claimed that following the defeat of the Nazis, the world was divided into two opposing camps. In the west, there were the capitalist regimes, and in the east, there were the communists.

Stalin was correct – the division of Europe had led to a breakdown in trust between east and west, and to a 'Cold War' in which the two sides continually spied on each other and anticipated the declaration of war. The Cold War allowed Stalin to maintain his control over the Russian economy and society under the banner of national defence. Moreover, the Cold War gave him the pretext to demand full cooperation from Communist leaders across eastern Europe in the name of security against a common enemy.

Economic superpower

Russia's superpower status was further enhanced by its powerful economy. Russia and America were clearly the economic forces of the new post-war world. In anticipation of military conflict with the west, Stalin deliberately created an economy that was geared to war. Indeed, Russia's economic might was essential to the new projects that would underline Soviet power in the Cold War era – the development of nuclear weapons and ballistic missiles.

The Fourth Five-Year Plan

The priority of the Fourth Five-Year Plan was heavy industry. Production in heavy industry had significantly decreased during the Second World War. For example, steel production in 1945 was at 45 per cent of its 1940 levels, while pig-iron production was only 26 per cent of that achieved in 1940. The military were to be reconstructed due to the threat posed by the USA and its allies. Soviet planners allocated 7.4 billion roubles for defence spending in the first year of the new Plan. This compared with 5.7 billion roubles in 1940, the last year of peace prior to Russia's involvement in the Second World War.

Economic boom

The later 1940s and the 1950s were a time of continuing economic growth for Soviet Russia. Total industrial production by 1952 was double that of 1940. At the end of the Plan, in 1950, heavy industry had clearly recovered from the ravages of war. Steel production by 1950 was 49 per cent above the 1940 figure. Similarly, coal output was 57 per cent higher than 1940, cement was 75 per cent higher, glass was 90 per cent higher and electricity was 87 per cent higher. In each case, industrial production exceeded the targets set in the Fourth Five-Year Plan.

The focus on heavy industry and the military came at the expense of living standards. Indeed, from 1946 to 1951, conditions for the majority of Russians were worse than at any point during the 1930s. In terms of housing, for example, it is estimated that 50 per cent of Soviet accommodation was destroyed during the Second World War. The remainder was poorly maintained. In 1946, approximately 90 per cent of central heating systems in Moscow did not work. Moreover, the regime deliberately kept prices high and wages low to encourage women to stay in the labour force. Indeed, while the Five-Year Plan was consistently over-fulfilled in terms of industrial output, it failed to achieve the vast majority of its targets for consumer goods. The Fourth Five-Year Plan was designed to protect Soviet citizens from external invasion, but did nothing to address the hardships of daily life. Nonetheless, Russia's claim to being a superpower depended on its ability to wage war, and therefore living standards played little part in the thinking of Soviet economists obsessed with Russian greatness.

Military superpower

The USSR's status as a superpower was confirmed by the development of a Russian nuclear weapon. The American bombing of Hiroshima and Nagasaki changed modern warfare. Stalin realised that if the USSR was to survive, it had to manufacture an atomic weapon of its own.

The Soviet bomb project, led by atomic scientist Igor Kurchatov, quickly caught up with its American rival. First, this was due in large part to Russia's control over the Eastern bloc. East Germany and Czechoslovakia, which were both in the Soviet sphere of influence, had large deposits of uranium, the essential ingredient of the first generation of atomic bombs. Secondly, the Stalinist command economy was ideally suited to the task of weapons production. Gosplan was able to divert vast resources to the development

of nuclear weapons. Thirdly, the physicists involved were aided by Soviet spies who had access to American and British nuclear secrets. Fourthly, Soviet scientists were subjected to continual propaganda emphasising the importance of the project for world peace and the defence of the Motherland. Consequently, the scientists collaborated enthusiastically and were even willing to endanger their own lives in order to speed up research. Finally, Beria, Head of the NKVD and Stalin's most trusted henchman, was put in charge of the bomb project. As a result, the majority of nuclear scientists were never purged during the 1940s, and they enjoyed considerable intellectual freedom – an indication of just how significant the bomb was to Beria and Stalin.

RDS-1, the first Soviet atomic bomb, was tested in 1949 in a remote area of Kazakhstan. It had taken the Americans six years to develop the atomic bomb, whereas Russian scientists had achieved it in less than four. By 1953, Soviet scientists had gone one step further and developed the hydrogen bomb, the second generation of nuclear weapons. The first Soviet hydrogen bomb, codenamed 'layer cake', was tested in Kazakhstan in 1953 and proved to be ten times more powerful than the first generation of weapons.

The Soviet atomic tests were significant because they demonstrated to the world the awesome power of the Russian military. Essentially, they showed that Russia and America were equals in terms of their military technology. Soviet nuclear success guaranteed the survival of socialism in the USSR and eastern Europe, and created a military stalemate between the world's two superpowers.

Conclusion – a dysfunctional superpower

In 1929, Stalin had become the ruler of a backward, peasant country. The majority of Russians lived in the countryside and could neither read nor write. By 1953, Russia was a highly industrialised, urban nation, technologically advanced enough to create its own nuclear bomb. Russia's population were well educated and an entire generation of industrial specialists had been created under Stalin's rule. This, coupled with Russian victory in the Second World War and its superpower status following the war, seemed to prove that Stalin's policies had been correct. For these reasons, Stalin's prestige was higher than ever at the time of his death in 1953.

Nonetheless, Stalin had created a dysfunctional superpower. The Soviet Union's economic success in heavy industry was never matched in terms of consumer goods. Consequently, while the USSR was capable of creating atomic bombs, it was unable to produce enough footwear for its people. Additionally, continual terror forced Russia's people to praise the system and therefore stifled innovation and problem-solving. For this reason, under successive Five-Year Plans, the productivity of the Soviet labour force and the quality of manufactured goods remained lower than that achieved by western economies. Equally, the Soviet Union remained an insecure superpower. Stalin never believed that the Soviet people could be trusted with power. They were continually bombarded with propaganda, prevented from having contact with the outside world and terrorised to keep

Taking it further

Stalin was the most powerful man in Russia from the mid-1920s until his death in 1953. But he was never invincible. Indeed, there were several points during his career when he was vulnerable. Here are three examples:
- 1924 Lenin's Testament demands Stalin's removal as General Secretary of the Communist Party
- 1934 Congress of Victors – Kirov secures more votes than Stalin in the election for the Central Committee
- 1941 Hitler invades Russia – Stalin's foreign policy is clearly a failure; Stalin retreats to his private house, expecting to be arrested by Beria.

1. Using examples from your knowledge of Stalin's time in power, explain why his position was vulnerable at each of these points.
2. On which of these occasions was he most vulnerable? Explain your answer, referring to the wider situation in Russia at each point.
3. Can you think of any other occasions on which Stalin may have felt that his position was threatened?

them in order. Even contact with fellow socialists in the Eastern Bloc was discouraged. Finally, the Soviet Union was a superpower built on the slave labour of millions of prisoners from Stalin's gulags.

Postscript

Following his death, Stalin's body was put on display in Red Square in Moscow, beside the body of Lenin. However, Stalin's successors did not treat his reputation with such respect. Nikita Krushchev, who succeeded Stalin as General Secretary, broke the silence on Lenin's Testament, revealing that Lenin had never intended Stalin to be his heir. He went further, accusing Stalin of perverting communism. In the late 1980s, the Soviet government was forced to admit the scale of crimes committed during Stalin's rule. Finally, when Soviet communism collapsed, on 25 December 1991, Mikhail Gorbachev, the final leader of the Soviet Communist Party, announced the abolition of Stalin's 'totalitarian system', stating that it had 'deprived the country of becoming successful.'

Activity: Stalinism – 'Why wail over broken eggs when we are trying to make an omelette?'

At the time of his death, the Soviet media hailed Stalin as a genius who had successfully overseen the building of the world's first socialist society. However, western historians have disputed these claims.

1. One way to assess Stalin's success or failure historically is to compare his achievements with his aims. Use your knowledge and understanding of Stalin's time in power to complete, in detail, the following table:

Aim	Evidence of success	Evidence of failure
To maintain a socialist government in Russia		
Acceptance of socialist ideology by the Russian people		
For Communism to out-perform capitalist economies		
The extension of socialism throughout the world		

2. How far does this evidence suggest that Stalinism was a success?

    The achievements of Stalinism came at great cost. Millions died during forced collectivisation, the famine of the mid-1930s, the Great Terror and the Second World War. In response to early criticisms of Stalin's appalling violence, his henchman Lazar Kaganovich asked 'Why wail over broken eggs when we are trying to make an omelette?' Kaganovich's argument was that, in order to achieve great things, some people had to suffer.

3. To what extent do you agree that Stalin's successes were only possible with the accompanying human cost?

Skills Builder 4: **Extended writing**

So far, in the Skills Builders, you have learned about:

- The importance of writing in paragraphs
- Answering questions on causation and change
- How to write introductions and conclusions

Now you are going to learn about how to write a full response to an examination question. Remember you will only have 40 minutes for each answer so you need to make the most of your time.

Read the QUESTION PAPER thoroughly

You will have a choice of two questions on this topic, but you only need to answer one. Make sure that you make the right choice. Don't rush. Allow time – a few minutes – to decide which question to answer. You won't have time to change your mind halfway through the exam.

Read YOUR CHOSEN QUESTION thoroughly

Once you have made your choice, examine the question and work out what you are expected to do.

What is the question asking you to do?

There are a number of different types of question you could be asked. Examples are:

- How far
- How important
- How extensive
- To what extent
- Why

Make sure that your answer is relevant to the type of question that has been asked.

In the first four question types, you will be expected to assess a range of factors. You will weigh up the importance of each factor you mention in relation to the question. You will need to reach a judgement on the question in hand. For instance:

> (A) To what extent was the Great Terror the major reason why the USSR was unprepared for war in 1941?

In answering this question you will be expected to provide evidence of how and why the Great Terror was an important factor in Russia's lack of preparation for war. You will also be expected to assess the importance of other factors, such as Stalin's relationship with Hitler and Stalin's refusal to believe Soviet intelligence reports.

Make sure you cover the whole question

Here is an example:

> (B) How far do you agree that the USSR won the Second World War because of the mobilisation of Russia's people and economy?

In this question you must make sure that you explain both aspects of the question:

- They successfully mobilised the Russian people
- They successfully mobilised the economy

You will also be expected to assess these reasons for the Russian victory against other reasons, such as the Lend-Lease scheme and military tactics.

Make a plan

Once you are clear about what the question is asking, sketch out what you intend to cover. Write down what you think will be relevant information in the form of a list or a mindmap. Then organise your information in a way which best answers the question.

Writing the answer

Make sure that you:

- Write a brief introduction, setting out your argument and what you will be discussing in your answer.
- Write a separate paragraph for each factor/reason you give. In the paragraph, make sure that you make a clear point and support it with specific examples.
- At the end of each paragraph, make a clear link between the point you have made and the question, showing how the point answers the question.

- Avoid just writing descriptions.

- Avoid merely 'telling a story'.

- Write a concluding paragraph which sums up your arguments and provides a clear judgement on the question.

Pace yourself

Success in an examination is based partly on effective time management. If you have approximately 40 minutes to answer a question, make sure that after about 12 or 13 minutes you have written about one-third of your answer. And after 35 minutes you should be thinking about, and then writing your conclusion.

If you run short of time, make sure that you can still write a proper concluding paragraph. If necessary, you can save time by cutting short your treatment of the paragraph or paragraphs before, by:

- Writing the first sentence containing your point.

- Bullet-pointing your evidence for this point – the information that backs it up.

- Writing the last sentence of the paragraph which explains the link between your point and the question.

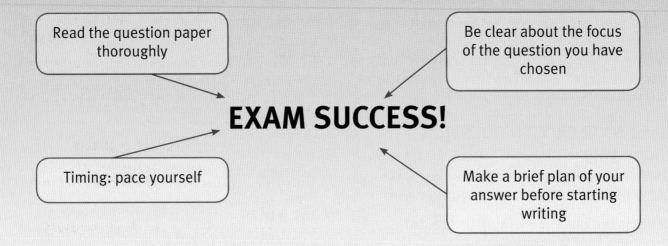

Activity: Write your own answer

Now write your own answer to this question, following the guidance given above:

> (C) How far was Russia's victory in the Second World War the major reason for the USSR's emergence as a superpower?

Examzone

Now that you have finished the course content, you will have to do the last bits of preparation for the exam itself. This advice covers two important elements for exam success: revising the information and using your information well in the examination

This topic – 'Stalin's Russia 1924-53'– is part of Edexcel's Option D: A World Divided: Communism and Democracy in the 20th Century, in Unit 1. The Unit 1 exam will be 1 hour and 20 minutes in length, and is worth 60 marks in total.

In the exam you will be given the choice of two questions on the topic Stalin's Russia. You will be expected to answer one of these and should spend no more than half the examination time answering it. You will also have to answer another question from a different topic. You will be expected to answer the questions you choose in essay form.

What to expect

You will need to remember information, but the exam is mainly testing whether or not you can apply the relevant information in answering a question. You will be assessed on your ability to recall and select historical knowledge and to deploy it (i.e. make use of knowledge to support your points). You can see that it's not just knowing what happened which counts, but understanding how to use what you know.

You will also be assessed on your ability to present historical explanations that show an understanding of history. You should read the question carefully to make sure you answer it in the right way. Sometimes questions will simply begin 'Why'. These are asking you to analyse the causes of an event or development. For the highest marks you will need to show how factors combined to bring about the event.

Most questions will ask you for a judgment. Here are some different types of question stems you may come across in the exam:

1. How far was x responsible for y?
2. To what extent did x change?
3. How far did x depend on y?
4. Did x play a major part in y?

Although judgment questions come in a variety of forms, they are all asking you to balance points. In the case of example 2 below, you will be looking for evidence of change and of continuity in order to reach a judgment about the extent of change.

When you choose your question in the examination, take note of what sort of judgment it asks you to make. The essay questions test a variety of skills. Here are some examples of different skills being tested by the questions.

- The analysis of, and judgment about, the **key features** of a situation.
  For example: *To what extent is it accurate to describe Stalin's social policy as 'the great retreat'?*

- The analysis of, and judgment about, the extent of **change**.
  For example, *How far do you agree that the Great Terror changed under Yezhov?*

- The analysis of **consequences** or **effects**.
  For example, *How accurate is it to say that the effects of the Great Terror on Russian society were entirely negative?*

- The analysis of, and judgment about, the **causes** of a historical event or situation.
  For example, *How far was he success of Russia's war economy responsible for Russia's victory in World War Two?*

Another type of question will ask you how far you agree with a statement. This is still a judgment question. You should clarify what the statement is about so that you know what the question expects of you:

- Is it a statement about causation, like this question: *How far do you agree that Stalin's position within the Communist Party was the main reason for his emergence as leader of Russia?*

- Or is it about , change like this question: *How far do you agree that Stalin transformed Russian society in the years to 1941?*

When you are clear about what the question wants from you, you can use what you have learned in the skills builder sections of this book to produce an answer based on extended writing (an essay) which will help you to gain high marks.

Examzone

How to revise

Make a revision plan

Before you start revising, make a plan. Otherwise it is easy to waste your precious revision time. It is helpful to look at your exam dates and work backwards to the first date you intend to start revising. Here are some tips on how to create a revision plan:

1   First, fill in the dates of your examinations and then any regular commitments you have. This will help give you a realistic idea of how much time you have to revise.

2   Plan your time carefully, assigning more time to topics you find difficult.

3   Use a revision 'checklist'. Look at what you need to know and try to identify any gaps in your knowledge.

4   Now fill in the timetable with sensible work slots and breaks.

5   Keep to this timetable! Organise yourself well and it will help you to fulfill your potential. If you have not prepared a revision plan yet, it is not too late to start. Put your plan up somewhere visible so you can refer back to it.

Revision tips

- Revise often – try to do a little every day.

- Make sure you have one day a week when you don't do revision or even think about exams – you'll come back to it refreshed.

- Take a 5- or 10-minute break every hour, and do some stretching exercises, go for a short walk or make a drink.

- Talk to your family or a friend about your revision – they may be able to help you. For example, they could test you on key facts.

- Keep bullet points on 'crib cards' highlighting important revision points. For example, you could have a list or a mind map of the reasons why Stalin became the leader of Russia. Use these for quick revision and for reading during 'dead' times – when you're waiting for a bus, for example.

- Use mnemonics. This is when you take the first letter of a series of words you want to remember and then make a new sentence. A common mnemonic for remembering the order of the points of the compass (North, East, South, and West) is 'Naughty Elephants Squirt Water'. You could use a mnemonic to help you remember the effects of the Great Terror.

- Some people revise well by listening, so you could try 'talking' your revision and recording it onto an mp3 player if you have one. Listen to these while lying in bed, while travelling in a car, or walking to the shops. This also takes the guilt out of being out and about rather than in front of your books!

- Practise your exam techniques. As you revise key topics, plan 5 or 6 points to make about the causes/ consequences/ key features / changes relating to major developments. You could use question stems 1–4 on the previous page, and slot in your own x and y.

- Try doing some timed essays. This will make it easier to write a good essay when it comes to the exam.

- Don't panic. Think about what you can achieve, not what you can't. Positive thinking is important! Remember the examiner will be looking to reward you for what you can do.

Assessment Objectives

To do well in your exam, you need to make sure you meet all the assessment objectives. Below are the assessment objectives you need to meet and some advice on how to make sure you meet them.

Recall, select and deploy historical knowledge
AO1a

In your essay, you must show that you can remember, choose and use historical knowledge.

- Remember – *recollect historical facts from your study of this unit*

- Choose – *select specific facts that are relevant to the essay you are writing*

- Use – *place these facts in your essay in a way that supports your argument*

Understanding of the past
AO1b (i)

You need to show that you understand the period studied. Simply telling the story of what happened will not help you to do this. Instead, you need to:

- Analyse – *break down the topic you are considering into key points*

- Explain – *suggest reasons why these key points provide an answer to the question*

- Reach a judgment – *Decide which of your key points was most important and provide reasons to support this*

As you think about analysis, explanation and judgment, remember to bear in mind the relevant **key concepts** and **relationships**.

Key concepts
AO1b (ii)

When faced with an essay question, consider which of the following key concepts it focuses on:

- Causation – *what made an event happen?*

- Consequence – *what were the results of this event?*

- Continuity – *in what ways did things stay the same?*

- Change – *in what ways were things different?*

- Significance – *why was this important?*

Then ensure that your answer remains focused on this concept.

Relationships
AO1b (iii)

Once you have planned the key points you will make in your essay, consider the following:

- How do these key points link together?

- Which key point was most important? Why?

Once you have considered these issues, arrange your points in an order that reflects the way they link together or the relative importance of each key point.

Level descriptors

Each essay you write in the exam will be given a mark out of 30 and will correspond to a level from 1 to 5, with level 5 being the highest. Here is some information about what the levels mean. Read it carefully and use this information to aim for the top!

Level 1:

- General points about the historical period that are correct but not necessarily focused on the topic raised by the question.

- The general points will not be supported by accurate and relevant specific examples.

Answers at this level will be very simplistic, irrelevant or vague.

Level 2:

- A number of general points about the topic of the question.

- The general points will be supported by some accurate and relevant examples.

Answers at this level might tell the story or part of the story without addressing the question, or might list the key points without backing them up with specific examples.

Level 3:

- A number of points with some focus on the question

- The points will be supported by accurate material, but some whole paragraphs may be either only partly relevant, lacking in detail or both.

At level 3 answers will attempt to focus on the question and have some strengths (some paragraphs will have point, supporting evidence and linkage back to the question), but answers will also have significant areas of weakness. For example, the focus on the question may drift, the answer may lack specific examples or parts of the essay may simply tell the story.

Level 4:

- A number of points which clearly address the question and show an understanding of the most important factors involved.

- The points will be supported by accurate material which will be mostly relevant and detailed.

- There will be clear explanation of how the points and specific examples provide an answer to the question.

At level 4 answers will clearly attempt to tackle the question and demonstrate a detailed knowledge of the period studied.

Level 5:

- A number of points which clearly answers the question and show a thorough understanding of the most important factors involved.

- The points will be supported by accurate material which will be relevant and detailed.

- There will be clear explanation of how the points and specific examples provide an answer to the question, as well as an evaluation of the relative importance of the different factors or issues discussed.

Answers that are judged to be level 5 will be thorough and detailed – they will clearly engage with the specific question providing a balanced and carefully reasoned argument that reaches a clear and supported judgment.

Sample answer 1

How far do you agree that Stalin's Five-Year Plans (1929-1941) improved the Russian economy?

An answer given a mark in Level 5 of the published mark scheme

Stalin's Five-Year Plans undoubtedly improved the Russian economy in terms of heavy industry. However, from the point of view of the consumer or labour productivity, the Plans were considerably less successful. What is more, the Plans only partially succeeded in meeting Stalin's aims for war preparation and social mobility.

EXAMINER COMMENT

A good start with a clear focus on 'improve'. It is clear that the answer will examine points for and against the claim that the Plans 'improved the economy'. But the last sentence has moved away slightly – the question is not asking 'to what extent did Stalin's Five Year Plans achieve their aims?'

Heavy industry was the central focus of the first three Five-Year Plans. Consequently, industries such as iron, steel and coal grew enormously between 1929 and 1941. For example, during the First Five-Year Plan, the production of iron almost doubled from 3.3 million tons in 1928 to 6.2 millions tons in 1932. Magnitogorsk, which was constructed during the First Five-Year Plan, aided the trebling of steel production during the Second Five-Year Plan. Even under the chaotic conditions of the Third Five-Year Plan, heavy industry continued to grow, with coal production, for example, increasing from 128 million tons in 1937 to 166 million tons in 1940. In this way, the Russian economy improved massively, changing from a backward peasant economy at the end of the 1920s to a highly industrial economy by 1941.

EXAMINER COMMENT

Precisely selected information supports the student's claims about the growth of heavy industry

In terms of consumer goods, there was significantly less improvement. Compared to the NEP, none of Stalin's Five-Year Plans were successful from a consumer's point of view. Indeed, living standards were never high on Stalin's list of priorities. Urban workers had to make do with rations, whereas in the 1920s, food was freely available on the open market. Under pressure from Kirov and other moderates in the Politburo, improvements were made during the Second Five-Year Plan, and the period from 1934-1936 was known as 'the three good years'. Living standards did improve for Stakhanovite workers, Alexei Stakhanov himself was rewarded with his own telephone. However, few workers enjoyed these luxuries, and, following the murder of Kirov, Stalin reduced the emphasis on consumer goods. Clearly, the consumer economy only improved for the lucky few, while the majority were worse off than they had been in the 1920s.

EXAMINER COMMENT

Precisely selected information supports the student's point that there was limited improvement in terms of consumer goods.

The Five-Year Plans had only limited success in improving labour productivity. During the First Five-Year Plan, the majority of Russia's workers entered factories with little or no experience of modern industry. Equally, much of what was achieved during the Plans was achieved by the slave labour of workers in the gulag. In both cases, workers could hardly be expected to produce high quality goods. During the Second Five-Year Plan, incentives were introduced in order to increase labour productivity.

However, most workers were still working with primitive technology and therefore could not match the efforts of the few famous Stakhanovites. The absence of consumer goods and the huge pressure of official targets demotivated the majority of workers and therefore Stalin's economy consistently failed to raise labour productivity.

EXAMINER COMMENT

Precisely selected information supports the student's point that thee was limited improvement in labour productivity – and there is linkage of this to the previous point about the absence of consumer goods.

The Russian economy did improve in terms of social mobility, at least during the First Five-Year Plan. Between 1928 and 1932, the urban population trebled. What is more, workers who had factory experience from the 1920s quickly became factory managers and 'Red Specialists'. However, the government recognised that this 'quicksand society' was difficult to manage and therefore, during the Second and Third Five-Year Plans, they stamped out the labour free market. Indeed, in 1940, internal passports were introduced which effectively abolished social mobility. For this reason, although it is fair to say that there were initial improvements in terms of social mobility, these proved short-lived due to government fear of the free market.

EXAMINER COMMENT

This is another important test of 'improvement in the economy'. The point is well supported, but could have been better developed to explain just why social mobility is important to a strong economy.

Preparation for war was an ongoing problem from 1936-1941. There were efforts towards the end of the Second Five-Year Plan to increase military production. The Second Plan succeeded in increasing defense spending from 366 million roubles during the First Plan, to 2,080 million. Although spending increased further under the Third Five-Year Plan, Stalin's purges reduced this last Plan to chaos, as it robbed Russian industry of expert managers. Additionally, much of what was produced was of such low quality that it was practically useless, and on the eve of war, Russia was still along way from being ready.

EXAMINER COMMENT

Perhaps a sign of haste, but this last paragraph is not so clearly and explicitly linked to 'how far … improved'. Relevant information is included, but it is not clear what central and relevant point is being supported.

In conclusion, Stalin's Plans partially succeeded in improving the economy. Heavy industry grew massively, but on the other hand, consumer goods were always more scarce than they had been under the NEP. The war demonstrated many of the failings of the Plans. In order to increase spending on defense, Stalin further cut spending on consumer goods. What is more, Soviet industry, which was able to produce large amounts of military equipment, was never able to achieve quality due to the chaos of planning and the poor motivation of Soviet workers.

EXAMINER COMMENT

This response was awarded a mark in low Level 5 of the mark scheme [25-30 marks]. The student considers range of valid points which are well developed. This is a clearly focused essay with much detailed supporting information. It is particularly impressive because it consistently links back to the question. Furthermore, it is well structured as it deals with information in a thematic and coherent way. It is clearly worthy of a low Level 5 mark (25) in spite of some weaker passages. Better linkage of the last paragraph (before the conclusion) to the question would have moved the answer higher in level 5.

Sample answer 2

How far do you agree that Stalin's Five-Year Plans (1929-1941) improved the Russian economy?

An answer given a mark in Level 3 of the published mark scheme

Stalin introduced the First Five-Year Plan for political, social and economic reasons. Politically, he was fighting against Bukharin and the Right Opposition who were '150% NEPist.' Socially, the Five-Year Plan was a good idea because it favoured the working class, who were the Communists' main supporters. The economic reason why Stalin wanted to adopt the Five-Year Plan was because the NEP had caused the grain procurement crisis which meant that the government was having difficulty procuring grain.

EXAMINER COMMENT

This is not a good introduction. It is answering a different question from the one set. It would be quite a good introduction if the question were about why Stalin introduced the Plan, but that isn't the question.

In 1929, Stalin had the idea of building a big steel works called Magnitogorsk. He employed a quarter of a million workers who went to the 'Magnetic Mountain' to build a city that would be the largest steel factory in Russia. Shift-workers and prison workers worked around the clock to make the factory, which was a big success and helped to increase the production of steel and meant that the Second Five-Year Plan was over-fulfilled by 3%. However, Magnitogorsk was also a failure. Even by 1932, the workers who had gone to work at Magnitogorsk were still living in mud huts with no toilets or heating. Workers found the work so hard that on average they only lasted for 82 days, except for the forty-thousand prison workers who had no choice and had to stay.

EXAMINER COMMENT

The student has introduced some relevant information here and linked it to improvement and to failure – hence implying lack of improvement or limits to improvement. More marks would be gained if these comments were more developed to make the link to the question clearer.

During the First Five-Year Plan, Stalin realised that Russia's transport system wasn't good enough to cope with all of the industry that was made in the Plan. In the Second Five-Year Plan, Stalin took steps to improve the transport system. The transport system improved massively in the Second Five-Year Plan and big projects were undertaken. One project was completed by Alexei Stakhanov, who completed four times the amount of work of the average construction worker. Therefore, it is fair to say that the Five-Year Plans did improve Russia's transport network and therefore improved the economy.

EXAMINER COMMENT

This paragraph is properly focused on 'improvement', but the information to support the point is quite sparse – in what way was the 'transport network improved'?

The Second Five-Year Plan had some successes and some failures. For example, living standards rose between 1934 and 1936. Bread rationing ended in 1934 and meat and butter were also more freely available. Also, there was an increase in defense spending, which rose from 4% in 1933 to 17% by the end of the Plan. However, there were still problems with the Plan, such as the lack of spare parts for machinery, and after 1936, some essentials were not easily available, such as shoes. In the 1930s, 6,000 people queued for shoes in Leningrad.

EXAMINER COMMENT

The student is showing positive and negative aspects of the Second Plan – but a good answer would start with 'tests' or criteria for 'improvement' and measure the outcomes of the plans against these. We do not get a sense from this paragraph of what constitutes an 'improvement'. The student never makes it clear.

The Third Five-Year Plan increased production in heavy industry. This was very important because Stalin thought there would be a war. The production of coal, for example, increased by about 40 million tons from 1937 to 1940. The production of crude oil also rose during the Plan. However, Stalin's purges meant that Gosplan was very disorganised, and therefore the Plan was never even properly published, which meant that the economy was not properly organised. Clearly, this was not an improvement on the Second Five-Year Plan. Living standards were also affected as money was diverted from the production of consumer goods in order to make more weapons.

EXAMINER COMMENT

This is a better focused paragraph. We have criteria here for improvement – increased production – and we have criteria by which to assess the limits of improvement – organisation.

Overall, Stalin's Five-Year Plans did improve the economy. Heavy industry grew throughout all the Plans and people moved from the country to the city. Lots of people got new skills and rationing was ended. The Plans also prepared Russia for war.

EXAMINER COMMENT

This response was awarded a mark in high Level 3 of the mark scheme [13-18 marks]. This essay has many good features: it is generally well-focused, and it does contain some detailed supporting information. However, it lacks the explanatory links to the question. Additionally, there is no clear logic to the structure of the essay. Note that a new and important point – the movement of labour to the cities–is simply referred to in the conclusion when it has not been dealt with in the body of the essay. For these reasons, it cannot reach Levels 4 and 5. It meets the criteria for high Level 3 and was given 18 marks.

Index

Published by:
Pearson Education Limited
Edinburgh Gate
Harlow
Essex CM20 2JE

First published 2008
Reprinted 2008, 2009
ISBN 978-1-84690-305-2

Printed and bound in China (CTPS/02)

Indexing by Indexing Specialists (UK) Ltd

Picture Credits
The publisher would like to thank the following for their kind permission to reproduce their photographs:
(Key: b-bottom; c-centre; l-left; r-right; t-top)
Alamy Images: Andrea Jones 5; **Corbis**: Underwood & Underwood 15, 19bl; **Mary Evans Picture Library**: 48; **Getty Image**s: AFP/ Stringer 75; Hulton Archive/Stringer 14, 19tr, 21tr; Keystone/Hulton Archive 13, 19tc, 21tc; Time Magazine/Stringer 55; **David King Collection**: 22, 91; **Stanford University**: Deni, Viktor N/Hoover Institution Archives 52; **TopFoto**: 2006 Alinari 16, 19br; RIA/Novosti 71; Topham Picturepoint 12, 19tl, 21tl
Cover images: Front: **Corbis**: Sygma / Thomas Johnson
All other images © Pearson Education
Picture Research by: Kevin Brown, Sandra Hilsdon

Every effort has been made to trace the copyright holders and we apologise in advance for any unintentional omissions. We would be pleased to insert the appropriate acknowledgement in any subsequent edition of this publication.